Easy living

John Harris used to teach French in England. Then (with his 'beautiful, shy wife' who is really the co-author) he settled in a country district in the Languedoc. There, happy, bronzed, but worried about his waist-line, he lives by his wits, cultivates his vegetables, writes occasional articles for *le Monde,* translates, fishes, teaches and bottles his wine. Every summer the Harrises are besieged by Britons asking questions about this and that . . . Hence this book, which brilliantly fills the gap between the hotel and restaurant manual and the guide to architecture and scenery.

Easy living
in
France

How to cope with
the French way of life

JOHN HARRIS

ARROW BOOKS

Aux habitants de Lieuran-Cabrières,
avec respect et amitié.

Arrow Books Limited
17–21 Conway Street, London W1P 6JD

An imprint of the Hutchinson Publishing Group

London Melbourne Sydney Auckland
Johannesburg and agencies throughout
the world

First published in Great Britain 1982

© John P. Harris, 1981

This book is sold subject to the condition that it shall
not, by way of trade or otherwise, be lent, resold, hired
out, or otherwise circulated without the publisher's
prior consent in any form of binding or cover other than
that in which it is published and without a similar
condition including this condition being imposed on the
subsequent purchaser.

Made and printed in Great Britain
by The Anchor Press Ltd
Tiptree, Essex

ISBN 0 09 928770 6

CONTENTS

This book is for holiday-makers and people settling down for longer periods; for people staying in hotels, renting self-catering accommodation, camping or caravanning in France.

Everywhere is becoming much the same these days. But Britain and France are still very different countries. *Vive la différence!* It can lead to delightful discoveries and awkward problems. The innocent Frenchman, having arrived in a British town on a Saturday night, will be surprised to find the butchers and the *pâtisserie* (if any) closed the next morning. Similarly the Briton in France. He should know that he can buy a pound of steak and a freshly-made real strawberry tart on a Sunday morning, but less easily on Monday.

For many years we spent our holidays in France, and now we live there. "How much easier this is in France!" and "How exasperatingly difficult this is in France!" have been frequent cries. (To be fair, there have been more of the first than the second.)

France is more conservative in its way of life, more traditional, than Britain. Geography forbids us to call France insular, but it is certainly hexagonal, which seems to lead the French into doing things their own way, rather inflexibly, under the impression that it is the best way conceivable. Well, we are very happy living in a village in the Midi! We want our readers to be happy too.

If we tried to thank all the people, French, British, American and others, whose advice, suggestions and questions have made this book possible, it would take several pages. And not a day would go by without our realising we had left somebody out. We hope that the many people whose good nature we have imposed upon (especially those who kindly read sections in manuscript) will accept our apologies for not naming them here, as well as our sincere thanks.

Note : "we", in these pages, means me and my beautiful shy wife.

J. H.

The French

The French have been called selfish, grasping, mean, hypocritical, inconsiderate, self-satisfied and conceited. So have the British.

The inhabitants of our village, somewhere between Béziers and Montpellier, are kind, patient and friendly. They behave with natural dignity and good manners.

The point is that one must not confuse France with Paris... Paris is of course a wonderful place (especially when some great upheaval has deprived it of petrol and one can walk idly in the streets). One can be very happy there; it helps if one is fortunate in love, or has a lot of money. But big cities, packed with busy people intent on defending themselves against the less desirable aspects of modern life, are special cases. Paris is more crowded than London, but the rest of France has more space per person than Great Britain. Life can be pleasant and unhurried, in surroundings ugly only in easily escapable patches, in a climate which is quite often kindly, and where most people look reasonably happy.

We love our Parisian friends. These rare and cherished beings are stimulating, intelligent and generous with their time and trouble. But our fellow-villagers were an unexpected bonus. We thought we had simply found a decent house in beautiful countryside...

Some of the rules of the game are different in Paris. If you live for a while in rural France you may find the French rather diffident, cool or shy at first: they are weighing up whether you, as an *étranger* (i.e. someone born and raised more than ten miles away) are a sort of Parisian. You can prove your innocence by not being in a hurry; by not seeming to know better than the locals about how life should be lived; by saying *bonjour* with a smile, and shaking hands; by satisfying legitimate curiosity about who you are, where you are going today, where you have just come from, and what you are in the act of doing even if it seems obvious; and by asking local advice about important matters such as choice of restaurant.

Paris

In spite of all we say about France not being Paris, we hope that this book will be useful to people in the capital. After all, most Parisians have roots elsewhere in France, and return frequently to their native haunts; they may consider that real French life is un-Parisian, while being proud of the beauties and facilities of the city where they work. You cannot understand Paris without knowing how life is lived outside.

We have resisted the temptation to give specific information about Paris. Guide-books and other books about Paris, in English and in French, proliferate. The Briton spending a holiday in or near a village or small town is on his own. But in Paris, if he is on the tourist circuit there is a well-beaten path, and if he is settling for a longer period there are plenty of his fellow-countrymen who will show him the Parisian ropes. But if they know only Parisian Britons, he needs this book.

THE BRITISH COLONY COMMITTEE FOR PARIS AND DISTRICT (6 rue Halévy, 75009 Paris) publishes yearly a valuable *Digest of British and Franco-British Clubs, Societies and Institutions in France* — most of which are naturally in Paris. These include The Royal Society of Saint George (for the English), the Caledonian Society of France, the Paris Welsh Society, the Oxford Society and the Cambridge Society, all of which arrange various social events; and S.O.S. Help (the Samaritans — every day from 3 p.m. to 11 p.m. on 723.80.80). And many others.

Books, guides, maps

Guide books proper; literary works of great value; sheer waffle... about the geography, geology, history, topography, architecture (especially ecclesiastical), sociology, art, wines and what-not of France are to be found in profusion in British bookshops and in British public libraries. There are probably more good (and bad) books about France in English than in French. Many are brilliant; some are out-of-date; a few are cynical scissors-and-paste jobs repeating their predecessors' erroneous information.

Tastes and interests differ so widely, and books go out of print so easily, that we feel it would be foolish to attempt to give a bibliography here. We strongly recommend browsing in British public libraries (one of Britain's advantages - France is very poorly off in comparison) and bookshops before making any purchases.

For basic factual information the MICHELIN "GREEN" GUIDE BOOKS (not to be confused with the big red Michelin guide, of which more later) can be recommended. These cover the whole of France in 19 handy cheap booklets. Seven of these are available in English translations (Paris, Normandy, Brittany, Châteaux of the Loire, Périgord, Côte d'Azur, Provence). They are on sale everywhere in France, and give in a concise objective cut-and-dried manner the main things to know about the natural and man-made features of the area.

The annual edition of the big RED MICHELIN GUIDE is a different matter. Only if you are never going to look for a restaurant, sleep in a hotel or drive in a town can you afford to be without this magnificent work. It costs £5 or so. You will save some money if you buy it after you land in

France. On the other hand, you will not have had the opportunity of spending the evenings before departure making delicious gastronomic plans.

It does not list every hotel and restaurant in France, but it gives a liberal selection over the whole price range. The introductory pages (in four languages, including English) should be thoroughly mastered in order to get full value from the otherwise cryptic entries and symbols — a good hour's work, amply repaid. Test yourself! Opening the guide at random, you should be able to answer the following questions, among many others: will the hotel expect me to dine as well as sleep? will it accept cheques backed by my Eurocard? if there is a garage, is it free of charge if I have the current guide? does the price of the meal at the restaurant include service? and wine? if not, is there wine in carafe (cheaper than in bottle)? can I distinguish clearly the restaurant symbols for comfort; good food; good cheap food; and cheap food? where, on the town plan, is the garage which deals with my make of car? where is the market hall? can I dial direct (to England for example) from the telephone in my room, or does it have to go through the hotel receptionist?... (One does not have to know a word of French to answer any of those questions.)

If an establishment is mentioned, one can be reasonably sure that it is *sérieux* — that is, it does a sound professional job. If not, readers complain to Michelin, inspectors re-inspect (incognito) and next year the entry may be modified or removed. Michelin is reputed incorruptible.

The guide is revised and brought up to date every year. Even an old one can be useful, giving an idea of the *relative* prices of restaurants and hotels; and the very informative town-plans stay valid for a while. We get a new one every two or three years, and take free peeps in the book-shops in between (to see if any local restaurants have gained or lost a star, and how prices are evolving).

There are other guides to hotels and restaurants. The serious eater who reads French could supplement his

Michelin red guide with the annual GAULT ET MILLAU
guide. MM. Gault and Millau are gastro-journalists.
Their guide to restaurants and hotels covers fewer
establishments than Michelin, but covers them
descriptively, wittily and idiosyncratically, rather in the
manner of Britain's "Good Food Guide" but with greater
professionalism. (They have recently been getting rather
bored with *la grande cuisine traditionnelle*, but not all of us
have 500 or 600 restaurant meals a year, groaning at the
sight of yet another *tournedos Rossini*.) We have a good
deal of respect for G. & M., who also publish a monthly
food-and-travel magazine of some distinction. It could be
held that Michelin is reliable but tradition-bound,
whereas G. & M., being only a pair instead of a big
organization, are brilliant but patchy.

A good map for navigating across France is the small-
scale red Michelin map. But for any area where one
is going to stay put for a while, one should have the
appropriate MICHELIN "YELLOW" MAP (1 cm. to 2 km., or
about 3 miles to the inch). Although these are intended to
be motorists' maps, not walkers', they carry a lot of detail.
Any town or village whose name is underlined in red on
the yellow map has an entry in the red Michelin guide,
and any town that has a rectangle drawn round it has a
corresponding town plan in the red guide. Exit points
numbered on these town plans are similarly numbered on
the yellow map. For each town or village in the red guide
one is directed to the appropriate fold of the yellow map.
The maps are cheap, and are frequently brought up to
date. Beware of buying an old one (especially likely in
Britain) — the year of publication, in very small figures,
can be found near the top left corner.

See also LA CARTE DE BISON FUTÉ, page 31.

The INSTITUT GÉOGRAPHIQUE NATIONAL produces
excellent maps (scale 1 cm. to 1 km., or about 1½ miles to
the inch) which, like the Michelin maps, are on sale
everywhere in France. Cartographically, they are better

than the Michelin maps, especially for walkers. But they are dearer, and do not possess the advantage of tying in with the red guide.

Campers and caravanners will find the MICHELIN CAMPING GUIDE useful. It lists a wide selection of camp sites in all parts of France, with summary notes and four-language explanatory introduction. It ties in with the yellow maps and the red guide. A little study will thus enable one to find, say, a suitable site within striking distance of a temple of gastronomy or a restaurant renowned for the value of its cheapest menu, and where one can go fishing in pyjamas, straight from the tent, before breakfast.

Self-caterers will take their favourite cookery books. We suppose everyone has an Elizabeth David or two; if you haven't, now is the time to get your copy of her *French Provincial Cookery* — which really was made with love and care. If you are going to have a well-equipped kitchen and want to spend a lot of time at stove and sink, *Mastering the Art of French Cooking*, by Beck, Bertholle and Child, gives very clearly the full treatment of the main classical dishes. Both these are in Penguin as are Alan Davidson's *Mediterranean Seafood*, an amazing work (see page 76), and *Jane Grigson's Vegetable Book*; their authors are experts at having a delicious time in France.

A decent cheap cookery book in French is *La Cuisine de Mapie* by Mapie de Toulouse-Lautrec, in the paperback *Livre de Poche* collection. Full and reliable; not eloquent or readable in its own right, like Elizabeth David (or Jane Grigson) but giving the main recipes in the French house-wife's repertoire.

Soon after arriving in any town one should call at the SYNDICAT D'INITIATIVE (tourist information office). Its location will be shown on — of course! — the town plan in the red Michelin guide. Here one can get free leaflets on the town and region, and often large-scale street plans, better than ones on sale elsewhere. And one can find out when market day is — an important piece of information, both for business and pleasure, not given in the red guide.

Newspapers

British and other imported newspapers are on sale in larger centres, especially during the tourist season.

THE INTERNATIONAL HERALD TRIBUNE is an English-language daily, published in Paris. It costs about twice the price of a normal French paper. Linked with the *New York Times* and the *Washington Post*, it naturally has an American view of the world, devoting many of its pages to New York (and other) stock exchange prices, comic strips and baseball results. Outside Paris, it will be earlier with the news than imported papers.

Those who read French should not neglect the regional press. Local papers cover a wider area than in Britain, appear daily, and give the more important "foreign" news. They are of course invaluable as a guide to what is going on in the region — festivals, fairs, fêtes, weather, murders, accidents, demonstrations by irate farmers...

The "national" press is really the Parisian press, and plays a much less important role than its British equivalent. For those seriously interested in world affairs, who in Britain would take the *Times*, the *Telegraph* or the *Guardian*, there are LE FIGARO and LE MONDE. *Le Figaro* is more or less like British papers, and is said to have a right-wing bias. *Le Monde* is accused of right-wing bias by the extreme left, of left-wing bias by the extreme right, of excessive discretion by sensationalists, and of sensational indiscretion by the government. Of repellent aspect, it is nevertheless worth attempting, especially when anything important (*not* murders etc.) has happened anywhere in the world and one wants a serious full account, with necessary background information. Outside Paris it is later with the news than other French papers. This is because it is published in Paris in the afternoon, when it carries the following day's date. So the "Friday" paper is really Thursday's (and is referred to in the pages of *le Monde* as "Thursday's paper, dated Friday"). Despite this and other excruciating habits, there is nothing quite like this apparently stuffy journal on either side of the Channel, and one can become an addict.

A further word on the subject of French journalism. "Elegant variation" disappeared a long time ago as an English stylistic device; oysters no longer turn up as *delicious bivalves*. But in our local paper if *choux-fleurs, canards, truffes* or *l'or* are mentioned in line 1, they will inevitably become *inflorescences, palmipèdes, délicieux cryptogames* or *le métal précieux* in line 3. In a typical *le Monde* article on French politics, M. Michel Rocard will be referred to as *M. Michel Rocard, le député des Yvelines* and *le maire de Conflans-Sainte-Honorine* in rotation. *Le Monde* itself tends to be *le quotidien de la rue des Italiens* or *le grand quotidien du soir*.

France-Inter, the radio station, broadcasts brief news programmes in English, aimed at the tourist and motorist in France (news, weather, road conditions, festivals etc.) at 9 a.m. and 4 p.m. during June, July and August.

The language

Is your French rather shaky? Fear not. At school one may have been terrorised by the subtleties of the agreement of the past participle, or the subjunctive. But in speech such things cannot usually be heard anyway (almost all past participles sound alike, whether they are masculine or feminine, singular or plural) and it is amazing what liberties are taken, *in speech*, with the rules one had to learn in the old days. One's teacher may have made one translate such complexities as "I regret that we did not gather the tomatoes before it rained", but any normal person would say something like *O mon Dieu! Il pleut! Et les tomates!* — and would back away in fear and trembling at the sound of *Je regrette que nous n'ayons pas cueilli les tomates avant qu'il ne plût.* Quite right too — that sort of thing was for the mandarins of literature, years ago.

Communication is the thing. Two or three basic tenses of half a dozen basic verbs, a lot of common nouns and uninhibited gesticulation will work wonders, if one last "did" French long ago to the tune of "could do better if he tried". Genders? Unlike the agreement of the past participle, these can often be heard, and so most French people get most of them right — but they don't mind at all if one gets them wrong. If one is really sensitive about genders, asking for *un peu de...* or *un kilo de...* or *cent grammes de...* or *pour dix francs de...* (instead of *du...* or *de la...*) avoids showing one's hand. Better, however, to shake off all guilty feelings, especially if one is on holiday. After all, most French people under 40 have been subjected to a lot of English at school, so when one spares their blushes by talking some sort of French to them, they are duly grateful. Or ought to be.

The French love talking. They quite like listening, for short periods. But they just hate writing any sort of letter.

The average Briton — bureaucrat, shopkeeper, friend — will scribble something and post it. The average Frenchman has been thoroughly indoctrinated at school in the beauties of his language, the difficulties of its spelling and the importance of making a rough copy. In English, one either knows, or doesn't, how to spell *necessary*. In French, not only are there a dozen ways of spelling the word pronounced *donner*, but every Frenchman remembers that he has been taught how to work out the right way by the logical application of grammatical rules, and almost every Frenchman knows that if he had paid more attention and been brighter and better, he would remember them now. So he hesitates to put pen to paper. Few, even, of the top one per cent of the population will write a quick note; they wait until they can settle down to composing an elegant epistle. Go and see your man, or phone him!

If you know no French at all you can still have a good holiday. Learn quickly *bonjour monsieur, bonjour madame, merci* and *au revoir*, use them far more often than might be thought necessary, use gestures and mime without inhibition, and smile. This will go a long way. A big family of Australians, knowing no more than that, spent three months (their summer holiday in our winter) in our village. They had a wonderful time. All the locals enjoyed communicating with them. The Australians got to know some French (especially the children) and the villagers got to know some Australian. More important, they found out that the Australians were decent friendly people, interested in what goes on in a wine-producing village, who respected its inhabitants and weren't shy of sharing a laugh over a bottle of the product.

But one has to be able to deal with the numbers. Figures are fortunately international, as far as print goes (and the oddly deformed shapes shown by pocket calculators). The landlord (who wants to make sure you know what the rent is) and the vegetable-seller in the market will always be willing to jot down the figures. As these hand-written figures will look somewhat different from what one is used to, specimens will be found below.

0 1 2 3 4 5 6 7 8 9

When writing down figures, *cross the sevens*. Otherwise your seven may be taken for a one, French style. No need to make any other changes, except to remember that the French for a *decimal point* is UNE VIRGULE — a comma. Thus "three point one four two", as written by a Frenchman, looks to us like "three thousand one hundred and forty-two".

An ANCIEN FRANC is a centime. Some people still call centimes francs... No problem, really. See page 61. "Two francs fifty centimes" is written 2,50 F.

3,142
three point one four two

three thousand one hundred and forty-two
3.142

Essential
technical vocabulary

ENGLISH-FRENCH
the thingummy: le machin, le truc
the whatsit: le truc, le machin.

FRENCH-ENGLISH
le machin: the thingummy, the whatsit
le truc: the whatsit, the thingummy.

Do not confuse *le machin* with *la machine* — the latter means "the machine" (only).

Believe it or not, the above will get you a very long way. We once spent half an hour looking up the precise term we needed, to ask for some tool at the *quincaillerie* (perhaps it was a half-nurdled sproozling iron). Blank incomprehension. Then, with appropriate gestures, we asked for *un machin qui fait comme ça.* The tool was at once produced, with *Mais enfin, vous parlez très bien le français!*

If, when motoring, you find there is *un machin qui fait clic-clic-clic dans votre truc,* tell the mechanic that, and he will understand perfectly. So will the doctor, if it is you instead of the car.

Un truc (but not *un machin*) can also be abstract — a dodge, trick or knack. The *truc* shown on this page is worth several of those *machins* they use for money in Britain.

Motoring

Driving on the right

Driving in France is easier and pleasanter than driving in Britain. Most of the time. After the first few anxious miles, if one has never driven on the right before.

Having the steering-wheel on the "wrong" side is a good set-up for cautious driving. A few Swiss drivers buy cars like that, and some big Italian lorries are similarly equipped. It can be held to be preferable to be sitting nearer the precipice (or pavement, or ditch, or pedestrian) rather than having to estimate one's clearance from the normal driving position.

A co-operative passenger is useful — not to tell one to overtake, since that is the driver's responsibility, but to give early warning that oncoming traffic is making it pointless to edge out further.

One should have external mirrors on both sides of the car, and remember that the far one leaves a bigger blind spot than the near one.

Even with a very cautious approach to overtaking, one will often find that one makes better time than in Britain, since really slow lorries and really steep gradients are rarer, and traffic is less dense except during the "lemming" week-ends in July and August.

There are only two other major driving-on-the-right problems. The first is at roundabouts. In the absence of any other system of signalization (signs, traffic lights) the normal system of giving way to traffic coming from the right prevails (see PRIORITÉ À DROITE, below), demanding on roundabouts a totally different technique. In Britain one gives way to traffic already on the roundabout, and waits on the approach road, whereas, with *priorité à droite*, traffic on the roundabout should give way to allow other cars to enter. One would expect chaos, since there is likely to be less "waiting space" on the roundabout than on the approach roads. But a snarl-up rarely happens, since at busy junctions there will be traffic lights, or "give way" signs on some of the approach roads.

Some places (Quimper, for one) have recently been experimenting with priority-on-the-left roundabouts (thus producing the British-type situation, where one waits to get on the roundabout). But there are clear signs to show who gives way. *Priorité à droite* applies only in the absence of other indications.

The other problem is to avoid thoughtlessly reverting to driving on the left. The good driver should never assume that he is immune to this appalling aberration. It has happened to us twice in twenty-five years (well, once; the other time was driving on the *right* in a Devon lane after a good French holiday). That is far too often. It is unlikely to happen in heavy traffic, or on any road where other cars are setting an example. It can occur on narrow deserted roads, where one is driving more or less in the middle. Then the sudden appearance of an oncoming car, also more or less in the middle, may produce the wrong reflex. When one has pulled over to the left (at a petrol station, for example) there may be a tendency to stay on the left as one starts off again; or on entering a wide empty road from a narrow lane...

If one trains one's children to chorus "Drive on the right!" every time one starts up, it will become a shocking bore, one may be tempted to shriek "Shut up, I know!" and it should be a superfluous reminder 999 times out of 1 000. But if it prevents that one-in-a-thousand chance of acute embarrassment or heartbreaking disaster it is worth putting up with.

Cars can easily be hired in France (if you have your British licence with you) at about the same cost as at home. Try to avoid taking delivery in a busy town centre at the rush hour, if you have never driven a car with the steering-wheel on the other side before — it takes a little while to get used to. One can find oneself over-compensating: turning right when one's navigator says "turn left"... which may, of course, be the right thing to do if that person has got into a similar state of left-right reversal. Sorting this out in central Paris at mid-day can put a strain on a relationship. There, if one gets in the wrong traffic lane or changes one's mind at a junction, it is more restful to have the steering-wheel on the British side — one's companion, sitting in the expected position for a French driver, may (with luck) take the first full flow of the other driver's eloquence before smiling sweetly and saying "Look, no hands!".

Priorité à droite

In Britain almost all intersections without traffic lights have signs saying who gives way to whom. One gets so used to this arrangement that in remote country districts where there are no signs one assumes that traffic on a road that goes straight on has priority over anything coming out from side roads.

In France a different system prevails. In the absence of any indication to the contrary, TRAFFIC COMING FROM YOUR RIGHT HAS PRIORITY, and traffic coming from your left should give way to you. (This explains the roundabout situation mentioned earlier.)

France is more than twice as big as Britain, with many more roads. In the good old days, when far fewer French people had cars, the system could be left to look after itself. There was no need to erect signs at junctions. But nowadays it is no longer an event to see another horseless carriage, and *indications to the contrary* are frequent. No problem for the Briton: "give way" signs, STOP signs and traffic lights are more or less the same as at home. THE YELLOW SQUARE is however a novelty. It means that you are on a priority road. Traffic, both from right and left, should give way to you, having passed "give way" or STOP signs before joining your road.

A more important sign, from the point of view of safety, is THE YELLOW SQUARE WITH A BLACK BAR. This means that your road no longer has priority, and you must (in the absence of indications to the contrary) revert to the *priorité à droite* system. This might be just before your road merges with another ex-priority road; then, after the junction you should see the un-barred yellow square again. Or you may lose priority just before a town or village. You don't lose priority for all towns and villages.

The signs are big and clear, and it is wise to notice them, so as to know if you are supposed to screech to a halt when something shoots out from a little road on the right, and to understand why the driver behind hoots indignantly when you give way unnecessarily.

In theory (but the status of roads can change after maps went to press) red roads on the Michelin maps are priority roads. This is useful for planning, but maps are not evidence. You should know the status of your road from its signs.

It would be a pity to restrict even long-distance journeys to main roads or motorways — especially motorways, since they all look much the same, whether near Birmingham, Gelsenkirchen or Châteauneuf-du-Pape, and French ones cost money that could be better spent in a cheerful little restaurant, lunching under the trees by the river, just off a quiet country road. Secondary roads (yellow on the Michelin maps) carry less traffic, may take one through pleasant places, and can prove as fast as more important roads. But they do tempt one to potter slowly, and even stop and stare.

While on the subject of roads, it is worth reflecting that in Britain and France there are approximately the same number of accidents per year, but considerably more people are killed in France. This seems odd at first sight, since the French have more roads but about the same number of cars. The reason perhaps lies in the emptier roads. If you have to crawl along, you can't do so much damage if you hit someone... Recent accidents in our little area of France have been caused by zooming along on apparently clear roads, and suddenly, over the brow of a hill or round a curve, meeting another driver doing the same. Motoring has to be tolerated for the freedom and convenience it brings. It can be a pleasure in France, where there are only about 100 people to the square kilometre instead of Britain's 230, but getting *fun* out of an activity that kills and maims thousands every year is overdoing it. The French are abandoning *la conduite sportive* in favour of prudence.

Road signs

Road signs are nowadays international, more or less, and your motoring organisation will have briefed you. One or two are worth comment.

BETTERAVES are sugar-beets and mud on roads in the harvesting season. Only in the north.

VENDANGES is the southern (and more cheering) equivalent. At vintage time (end of September, October) you may see this sign near *caves coopératives* (wineries). Trucks, vans, trailers, trundling around laden with tons of grapes and tired but happy peasants. Go slow, and wave!

GRAVILLONS: loose gravel; and almost certainly the remains of windscreens by the side of the road. Finishing off a road with loose chippings and then leaving time and traffic to remove the surplus is a French habit which has not yet died out. At the end of a stretch of this sort of thing garages triumphantly advertise POSE DE PARE-BRISE (windscreens fitted). Convenient, if one has a popular model of car. Otherwise one of those plastic temporary things is handy. Instinct urges one to go fast, avoiding being overtaken and sprayed with projectiles. It can be shown mathematically that this is wrong. An air-borne *gravillon* has negligible speed; it's the speed you hit it with that counts. (Mustn't exaggerate. We have done about 150,000 miles in France, and the same in Britain, and have lost one windscreen in each country.)

CHUTE DE PIERRES: the sign seems to suggest the imminent descent of a massive boulder. Don't look up at the mountain-top; it may never fall, and if it does one might as well take it philosophically, with British phlegm. Look at the road surface instead. The sign means that stones may have got there.

TOUTES DIRECTIONS means "all directions", thus causing mild amusement. The other direction is usually CENTRE VILLE (town centre), TOUTES DIRECTIONS being for through traffic.

POIDS LOURDS are heavy lorries. On signposts, the name of a town (etc.) with the words POIDS LOURDS means that that is the way *they* should go, but you need not.

A GREEN SIGN rather like an arrow but more like a coffin on its side indicates an alternative route to some distant destination, recommended for holiday traffic at busy times — longer and off the main roads, but possibly quicker if the main roads are crowded; and probably pleasanter. The ultimate destination is indicated in white lettering on a green background.

Similar signs, but with the name of the destination in BLUE on ORANGE background, indicate *un itinéraire de délestage* — a short alternative route for avoiding likely bottle-necks.

In the past few years, LA CARTE DE BISON FUTÉ has been available free at petrol stations in the holiday season. It is a map showing the alternative routes mentioned above. Useful. *Bison futé*, or Wily Buffalo, is a redskin who knows when the palefaces will be on the war-path — a dream-child of the French Ministry of Transport.

Speed limits

90 k.p.h. (about 55 m.p.h.) in general.

60 k.p.h. (about 37 m.p.h.) in built-up areas (AGGLOMÉ-RATIONS) except when there are signs showing a different limit. You enter *une agglomération* when you meet the sign showing the name of the town or village in dark blue lettering on a white background. You leave it when you meet a similar sign with a diagonal red stripe across the name. The existence of street lighting has nothing to do with the matter.

110 k.p.h. (about 70 m.p.h.) is allowed on dual carriage-ways if there is a sign to that effect.

130 k.p.h. (about 80 m.p.h.) is the maximum on motorways.

Many French drivers go rather faster than the above maximum speeds. Well, it's their country... And their police do sometimes catch them. You can infuriate a wicked Frenchman behind you by finding a stretch of road where overtaking is forbidden and driving along it at the maximum permitted speed while making it difficult for him to overtake you. As infuriated bad drivers are a public danger, we have reluctantly abandoned this game.

Seat belts - children

The law says that seat-belts must be worn in front seats, and that children under 12 must sit at the rear.

Fines

For minor offences, the police will kindly allow you to pay a smallish fine (UNE AMENDE FORFAITAIRE) on the spot. You should be given a receipt. If you consider yourself innocent you need not pay. The subsequent legal proceedings will provide an expensive but interesting experience.

Accidents

Your insurers or motoring organization should have provided you with duplicate forms (CONSTATS À L'AMIABLE) in the two languages, to be completed with the co-operation of the other driver.

Your car

The A.A. and the R.A.C. have all kinds of up-to-date information and services for the motorist going to foreign parts. But a word on choice of car. We do not suggest that you need a special car for your French trip. But if you are going to make a habit of holidaying in France, or are about to go there for a long stay, and if the time has come for a change of car, then (other things being equal) there is something to be said for buying a French one if there is a reliable service station for that make near your normal home. There are very few British cars bought in France. The majority of Frenchmen run French cars. "Foreign" ones are mostly Italian, German or Japanese; one sees just an occasional Mini, Jaguar or Rolls under French registration plates. The result is that garages specially equipped to deal with British makes are few and far between (your red Michelin guide will tell you where they are). If you take a British car to France, take a selection of spare parts, and profit from the A.A.'s or the R.A.C.'s willingness to fly out the ones you didn't take, and to make arrangements for you if your car has to be left behind. But if you have a popular French model, almost any one-man-and-a-boy garage will keep you mobile.

As you motor in France you will discover why French cars have more supple suspension and softer seats than British ones. France has more roads, Britain has (usually) better road surfaces. The sign CHAUSSÉE DÉFORMÉE (*bumpy road*, or perhaps *temporary road surface* — but the realistic French don't call it temporary) is all too frequent, except of course on motorways. Many a powerful British car, jolting along at about 35 m.p.h. because the occupants don't want to be shaken to pieces, has been overtaken by horrid little Citroen 2CVs (the ones that look like upside-down tin prams). These, having taken about ten minutes to wind themselves up to 60 m.p.h., sail past swaying gently up and down on their magnificent suspension; they were designed to enable peasants to transport baskets of eggs across stony wastes and down pot-holed tracks.

We cannot resist a further word on the 2CV, mainly for those about to settle in France who do not feel they have to keep up their standing by driving a less inelegant vehicle. There is a lot to be said for having one, *in France*, if only because the thing has been made in such large numbers for so long that any French garage can fix it, and spare parts (new and second-hand) abound. It has two tiny air-cooled cylinders, so that the French equivalent of the Road Fund Tax *(la vignette)* is peanuts (70 francs a year for ours, which is over 5 years old and going strong; if it were younger, the *vignette* would be 140 francs. The *vignette* for a 2-litre car would cost much more than in Britain — it goes by horse-power, but is halved when the car is five years old.)

Our 2CV once did 70 m.p.h. with the *mistral* behind it. In the opposite direction it might have reached thirty, in third gear. But — it has four doors, the back seat lifts out for bulky loads, the roof rolls back in the spring, the engine is said to last for ever even if the body rusts through, its big wheels, high clearance and extraordinary suspension take it over any surface, and its second-hand value is high (we bought it in London, with the steering-wheel on the French side, for about two-thirds of what it would have fetched in France).

If you settle in France with a car registered in Britain you don't need to bother about re-registration for a year or so — a modest saving on Road Fund Tax. You must of course have insurance on one side of the Channel or the other. For big engines (over 1000 c.c.!) French insurance is much dearer. After a year's residence the authorities will, if you wish, swap your British licence for an equivalent French one.

At the service station

Petrol is *essence* (*pétrole* is the crude oil that goes slurp slurp into the barrels). It comes in two grades, *essence (ordinaire)* and *super*.

"*Fill her up*" — FAITES LE PLEIN, S'IL VOUS PLAÎT.

"*50 francs' worth of super*" — POUR CINQUANTE FRANCS DE SUPER, S'IL VOUS PLAÎT.

"*Check the oil*" — VÉRIFIEZ L'HUILE, S'IL VOUS PLAÎT.

"*The tyres*" — LES PNEUS (the "p" is pronounced; the word rhymes with "fur").

And see "ESSENTIAL TECHNICAL VOCABULARY", page 24.

Trains

and *le compostage:* a warning

On many trains (luxurious and/or very fast ones) a special supplement is payable (and/or they are first class only). If you have bought your ticket and been briefed at a reputable travel agency, this will have been taken care of. Otherwise, study the time-table and the notices carefully, or you may be surprised when the ticket-inspector asks you to pay a supplement not covered by an ordinary ticket.

It is worth noting that a married couple can obtain, at major railway stations, a *carte couple* valid for 5 years, entitling one of the couple to a 50 % reduction on internal French railways fares, when they are travelling off-peak together. You don't have to be French, or permanently resident in France. All that is needed is evidence of being a married couple (passports will do) and — as so often in France — identity photographs. Unmarried couples (of different sexes) living together can also qualify, but they must produce some sort of evidence that they live at the same address.

A useful booklet in French, *Le guide pratique du voyageur*, can be obtained free at railway stations.

What follows does not apply to international train journeys, but to journeys that start and end in France, such as one might make for an outing by an interesting line.

A new system was introduced recently. You can buy your ticket whenever it's convenient, and wander on and off the platforms without having to show it or get it punched by anybody. But before you get on your train you must date-stamp it yourself, by sticking it into a special apparatus. (*Composter* means to date-stamp.) There are no ticket-inspectors at the stations, but plenty on the trains, and anybody who has not *composté* his ticket has to pay them a fine on the spot (variable with length of journey).

In the summer of 1978 Mr. Roy Plomley (he of "Desert Island Discs") bought two 9 franc return tickets, for a little trip from Cannes. He was very annoyed at being fined 40 francs for *non-compostage*, and wrote to *The Times* about it, threatening to boycott France if he didn't get his money back. He was especially indignant because notices about not sticking one's head out of the window, and about how to flush the lavatory, are in several languages, but the instructions about *compostage* are only in French. (He might have added that *composter*, a rare verb, does not figure in the usual bilingual pocket dictionary.) Cynics suggested that if foreigners get decapitated or fail to master the lavatory it is just a nuisance and there is no profit in it. *Le Monde* had a little article about how British Railways and the London Underground accept a gentleman's word. Eventually, Mr. Plomley did get his money back, and won't have to spend his next holiday on a desert island. The S.N.C.F. say they will consider having multilingual notices. But you have been warned. The point is that if a wicked man did not date-stamp his ticket, he could use it over and over again if an inspector on the train did not catch him.

Restaurants

Temples of gastronomy

If you want to spend £35 or more a head (1981 prices), there are a number of restaurants that will cheerfully cater for you. An outlay of this magnitude, perhaps made only once or twice in a lifetime, might as well leave one with the memory of a delightful evening rather than of a stupendous bill... so careful planning is called for, to avoid being charged wholly unjustified prices in an establishment run with the aim of soaking the rich. There were just twenty-one restaurants in the whole of France which were awarded three stars in the 1981 red Michelin guide. The introduction explains this rating as follows: *Here one will find the best cooking in France, worthy of a special journey. Superb food, the epitome of French cooking. Fine wines, faultless service, elegant surroundings... One will pay accordingly!* This is not gush. We repeat, there were only twenty-one of these, as against 80 two-star and 520 one-star restaurants in the 1981 Michelin guide — and thousands of unstarred ones listed which serve excellent meals (if they don't, they soon get removed from the Guide). The Michelin guide lists only a respectable fraction of the total number of restaurants in France — and, though really bad restaurants can be found in France, they are rare, in comparison with other countries which shall be nameless. The inspectors are ruthless and the stars are well deserved.

So, use your Michelin and perhaps your Gault-et-Millau (see Books pages 14 and 16). If they agree you can hardly go wrong. Then reckon up the probable cost, remembering that the price given in the Michelin guide for a meal in a 3-star restaurant is unlikely to be preceded by the symbol sc, for *service compris*, so you will need to

add about 15 % for service; and you will have to pay a
goodly sum for your wine; and your after-dinner euphoria
may lead you to order a round or two of the house's very
special cognac or some ambrosial liqueur not to be found
anywhere else, which will be no vulgar £1-a-shot fire-
water.

Then, book your table! About a fortnight's notice
should be enough, though if you are the Prime Minister,
or just perhaps the Leader of Her Majesty's Opposition
on a lucky day, a table might be found for you if your
bodyguard phones up early in the morning. You must
certainly abandon any notion of just dropping in — these
places do, in their way, offer good value for money, and
they are justly appreciated by the wealthier French gourmet. If they *aren't* fully booked, something awful may
have happened since the last Guide went to print —
beware!

Bargains

On the other hand, there are many excellent restaurants
in France where one pays surprisingly little for a delicious
meal, freshly cooked, decently served, and based on
honest home-produced ingredients. If one has gone to
market and bought the materials for a proper French meal
of hors d'oeuvres (say, a little ham, a slice or two of
saucisson, freshly grated raw carrot, celeriac and other
crudités) or home-prepared soup; then freshly fried whitebait, or a trout, or an omelette; then a *bœuf bourguignon*,
or roast veal, or a modest steak; then a vegetable course or
a plain lettuce salad freshly mixed; then a session with the
cheese board; then fruit or a simple sweet — at the worst a
factory-made ice-cream; with of course freshly baked
bread, and as much ordinary wine as one cares to drink;
and if one has cooked all this, and served it decently
(though perhaps asking one's guests to use the same knife
and fork for more than one course); and cleared away and

done the washing-up — if, as we were saying, one has done all this, one is somewhat startled to find that the little place round the corner charges only 40 francs, or even less, for the same (service included). But it is done, all over France. The answer is that these modest restaurants are family concerns. They pay no staff, and what they do about income-tax and T.V.A. (French V.A.T.) is not our business; grannies play a valued role behind the scenes, and the vegetables and the poultry may come from the garden. We have in fact given above the standard fare at our local small-town restaurant; the sole menu, at 42 francs, is often more enterprising, and the place earns its red R in the 1981 Michelin guide. The red R means that the restaurant offers, at a moderate price (wine, V.A.T. and service included), a particularly high standard of cooking. There are lots of "red R" restaurants, and they are not the cheapest: if you don't mind paper table-cloths, and the presence of a respectable lorry driver or two at the next table, you can find even better value. Michelin has another symbol for restaurants offering a decent meal for under 35 francs, but not of the exacting standard of food, service and comfort required for a red R.

All French restaurants display their menu outside. If you see a cheap menu, and the restaurant seems nearly full of Frenchmen and Frenchwomen, you are probably on to a good thing. French commercial travellers, and especially French lorry drivers, work long hours and appreciate a proper meal. Their presence is a good sign. If a small unpretentious restaurant displays the RELAIS ROUTIER plaque outside, it has been approved by the French lorry drivers' union, and in its way offers excellent value — a totally different atmosphere from that of Fred's Transport Caff. But of course you will not be in and out in half an hour, or anything like it (see SNACKS below); a two-hour break at midday for serious eating and chatting is fairly normal.

If you are looking for bargains, you must study the menu carefully. The things to look for are SERVICE

COMPRIS (service charge included) and VIN COMPRIS or
BOISSON COMPRISE (wine included; or a choice of wine,
beer or mineral water included).

At the restaurant mentioned above, which we will call
restaurant A, you have *service compris* and *vin compris*.
There is just the 42 franc menu (60 francs for Sunday
lunch, a superior menu) with a couple of choices for each
course; and 42 francs, neither more nor less, is what your
meal will cost you (at June 1981 prices). Well, coffee is
extra, and instead of the good local wine of which you are
given unlimited quantities, you can buy a more
impressive-looking bottle. Excellent value, though
perhaps too hearty for the holiday-maker who did not get
up at half past six with just a cup of coffee and a roll to
keep him working until noon. The Michelin guide will
have given this information, more or less, with its red R,
its SC and its BC.

Not far away is restaurant B, one of the 520 restaurants
that have one star in the 1981 Michelin guide. As this also
has the SC mention *(service compris)* and has menus from
55 to 150 francs, it looks as though one might get a better
meal here than at restaurant A, for little more money. Not
so! A study of the menus outside the restaurant shows
that the 55 franc menu is a perfunctory affair (it is in fact
inferior to restaurant A's 42 franc menu). But the
90 franc menu is truly beguiling on paper, and in fact, on
the table, turns out to be worth every centime of the
price: beautifully prepared, lots of choice, elegantly
served... they tie a little bib round your neck when you
attack your *écrevisses à l'américaine* (fresh-water crayfish
in a tomato-and-cognac sauce, after which the finger-bowl
is needed, since these things would present insoluble
problems with knife and fork). But your *vin* is not *compris*,
dear me no. You are charged 25 francs for a bottle of the
wine we can buy *en vrac* (in bulk — see page 97) at 3,50 F
the litre. So all in all a good meal at restaurant B will cost
nearly three times as much as at restaurant A. It is still
good value: they make their profit on the wine, not on the
menu. One had been warned — not only is there no BC in

the Michelin guide, but also no symbol for moderately-priced wine *en carafe*.

At the other end of the scale, we sometimes go to restaurant C, run by an Anglo-French couple (the French half does the cooking, but if you order well in advance she will produce a heavenly traditional steak-and-kidney pie). There, for 27 francs, you get one course fewer than at restaurant A; and a foil-wrapped piece of cheese instead of a go at the cheese-board (the latter can be a ruinous item for the restaurateur). A quarter-litre jug of drinkable wine is included; further jugs at 2 francs each. Portions are normal by French standards, generous by British ones, and the meal takes the usual hour and a half in quite agreeable surroundings. They do this twice a day, seven days a week, and are hoping to be awarded the *relais routiers* plaque soon. The restaurant is not in the Michelin guide. One can find small family restaurants doing this kind of thing all over the country.

VIN COMPRIS means that a carafe (or an unlimited supply) of ordinary wine is included in the price of the menu. There may be a choice of red, *rosé* or white. We recently witnessed a sad altercation between a restaurateur and a Briton who, with his forty-franc, fixed price, *vin compris* menu, had ordered a ninety-franc bottle of very superior white wine, served with pomp and circumstance in an ice bucket. The Briton expected to pay only forty francs for the lot... Both he and the restaurateur were understandably indignant.

If you want to have the "free" wine when you have chosen a *vin compris* menu, wave away the *Carte des Vins* (wine list) if they present it to you. Say firmly, "Je veux le vin ordinaire du menu."

Snacks

If what you want is a quick light meal, you will probably be frustrated. In Britain one can pop into a pub and have a couple of sandwiches during opening hours, or into a café; it is only after a certain time in the evening that one is condemned to hunger. In Italy there are bars everywhere, and nice roadside cafés, where an appetising *panino ripieno* can almost always be found — delicious little sandwiches with enterprising fillings; and in Italian restaurants one can have just a plate of spaghetti and a green salad, and be out again half an hour afterwards. In Spain there are *tapas* for recreational nibbling at odd hours...

But on the whole such frivolities are not to be found in France. The general practice is as follows: breakfast is a light affair, basically *café au lait* with bread, butter and jam, or croissants (this can usually be obtained at a café anywhere). The working French will have had theirs at seven or earlier, since the working day usually starts at eight. Twelve o'clock is the sacred hour. From half past eleven you should substitute *"bon appétit!"* for *"au revoir!"*. At twelve, serious eaters (who have *not* kept going during the morning on coffee and biscuits as on the other side of the Channel) sit down with eagerness and conviction to an hour or longer of conscientious consumption of conscientiously prepared food. This will keep them full of calories until about eight in the evening, when a somewhat lighter meal will complete the day's intake. (No tea-breaks, except for children.) In general, it is difficult to escape from this pattern, if one is not going to do one's own catering. The French, as we have said, are at least as traditional and conservative as the British. As in Britain, the eccentric foreigner who wants to behave in outlandish ways gets little co-operation from the natives.

But it is wholly conceivable, and not really sinful, that

one should want sometimes to carry on driving through the lunch hour, when the roads are empty, and then to spend twenty minutes and a few francs on something light; or that one should be visiting an interesting place and not want to sacrifice a couple of hours to the eating ritual. What can one do?

It is true that a number of ordinary cafés can produce a sandwich. But the French sandwich is unworthy of that great nation — or rather, it is a punishment for not taking proper meals with proper high seriousness. It is a cylindrical chunk of French bread, some 3 or 4 inches in diameter, split lengthways, with a chunk of ham or *pâté* or cheese in the middle. It is impossible for the human mouth to open wide enough to bite through it in one go. One can try flattening it, but one usually ends up by taking it apart and breaking off convenient morsels. Lord Sandwich turns in his grave.

The best solution is to pray successfully for fine weather. This will permit picnicking, and France is a lovely country to buy a picnic in. Your car, or your shopping bag if you are on foot, should contain at least a good sharp knife, some spoons, a cork-screw, a bottle opener, a few paper cups and some paper napkins. Well before twelve o'clock you spend happy moments at the *charcuterie*, the *boulangerie*, the *pâtisserie*, the *épicerie* and the fruit stall. There will be splendid temptations at the *charcuterie* — interesting little salads in plastic barquettes, pies, *pâtés,* cooked dishes such as paëlla, as well as all the hams and salamis. Outside there will probably be chickens roasting on electric spits, to be popped into neat insulated paper bags. As the Lord made chickens to be eaten in the fingers, and man made paper napkins to clean up with afterwards, nothing could be more suitable for lunching on hill-top or in city park. A bottle of wine, a bottle of mineral water, perhaps a litre bottle of table beer (just as good as in the little bottles, and very cheap)... There is no problem in fine weather.

Apart from picnicking, the tourist away from his base does have a few resources. On an earlier page we described the general pattern of eating in France. But there are just a few chinks in the system. Snack bars can be found in the centre of large towns, and some may serve something outside normal eating hours. Hamburger joints have recently been observed. Large towns may also boast a *salon de thé*, where fat ladies eat cream cakes. There are a few self-service cafeterias, often located in out-of-town hypermarkets. For example, when our friends land, hungry, at Montpellier airport at 2 p.m., the bar stocks nothing worth eating except a bag of crisps, and the restaurant (expensive) is packing up. But 3 or 4 miles away, on the way home, is the Casino supermarket, with its self-service cafeteria, open from 11 a.m. to 10 p.m., serving acceptable food in decent surroundings. It has therefore become a ritual to take the new arrival there, and feed him on a freshly grilled steak, with chips and a quarter bottle of champagne. Would there were more places which permit this at all hours!

There are also the motorway service areas, where snacks of a kind can be got outside normal hours, though of course less satisfactorily than in countries where snacking forms part of the pattern of life. And on the motorway one can picnic successfully: there are picnic areas with tables and benches (and lavatories and running water).

Cafés

The café is an admirable institution. Of course, it isn't what it was. Television in every home has killed it as a place of regular social attendance. But after the normal British scene, one rejoices at being able to sit in the sun (or the shade) on a pavement terrace with a glass of light beer, watching the world go by while one's family consumes coffee, lemonade from a freshly-squeezed lemon *(citron pressé)*, ice-cream and what-not; though Andy Capp would regret losing his refuge from the wife and kids.

The impecunious (and even the moderately pecunious) traveller soon learns however to treat the café with discretion. Teachers of French at British schools are only too used to the wail: "Oooh Sir! I went to a café in Paris and had a Coca-Cola and a bun and they charged me £2!" Investigation usually shows that the child in question had been sitting at a terrace table on the Champs-Élysées, where what one is paying for is a ring-side seat at the great spectacle of fashionable life (and a lot of traffic). To occupy this privileged position for a couple of minutes while slaking one's thirst makes as much sense as taking a box at the opera just to have a ten-minute quiet sit-down. We are MEAN: we go to one of these places (for a small black coffee) if what we really want is to stay there for at least an hour, talking, reading, meeting people, using the elegant lavatory accomodation, looking at the passing show and getting our money's worth. The schoolboy — if all he wanted was a little something to keep him going — should have bought a bottle of coke and a bun at the *épicerie* round the corner, and consumed them on a bench. In Britain there is little difference between the price of beer at the pub and at the off-licence; but in France you can pay anything from 4 francs to 14 francs or even more for a quarter-litre bottle at a café (depending on location and elegance), as against 2,60 F for a litre bottle at the *épicerie*.

So, if driving through France with a car-full of spouse and children, the rule should be: no stops at cafés just because someone is thirsty. There should be a prudent supply of litre bottles of lemonade and table beer in the car (kept if possible in an insulated box — many *épiceries* have bottles ready chilled). This keeps the offspring from dehydration more cheaply than in England. (Keep the bottles — there's a deposit on them; hand them in when you next stock up.)

Café stops should be made when a longish break seems desirable. One's table at the café becomes the rendezvous point for those who want a short stroll or a shopping expedition, and no doubt the café's sanitary facilities will be explored (prudent to be armed with a few sheets of one's own toilet paper). One item per head is our maximum. In ordering, *un café* means a small black coffee. A "white coffee" is *café au lait* or *café crème* — dearer than black.

A *panaché* is a nice drink, especially for medium-sized children who want to feel grown-up: a half-and-half mixture of beer and lemonade (a shandy, in fact), almost non-alcoholic. *Une pression* is a glass of pressurised keg beer. Beer, by the way, is generally considered a non-alcoholic drink in France. When one tells them that Britons succeed in getting drunk on it, they tend to say: "But they must have to drink *several glasses*!" Indeed...

In the south, a PASTIS is welcome in hot weather. *Pastis* is Pernod, Ricard, etc. — that greenish aniseedy liquid that turns cloudy (like Dettol) when water is poured into it. Although bottles of the stuff are expensive, it is a cheap drink in cafés, largely because it is very popular and served in very small doses. It comes with a lump of ice and a jug of water, and a pleasant and not really intoxicating half-hour can be spent diluting, sipping and re-diluting.

Do not order whisky! Although bottles of whisky (some in mysterious brands) cost about the same as bottles of *pastis*, the café charges four times as much — it is a show-off sort of drink (and served in large shots).

This book contains no vocabulary for interpreting café lists and restaurant menus. Firstly, quite good phrase books are easily obtainable, and go as far as they can be expected to; and secondly, it's a hopeless task. A good English book on French cookery is more to the point, since the names of the things *are* French anyway. What is the English for *pâté*, for example? Paste? Meat Loaf? Ugh!

As the French take food and drink seriously, and are not shy about doing so, very few waiters or customers will take offence if one points to something interesting that someone else is eating and asks, "*Pardon — qu'est-ce que c'est que ça?*" (Excuse me — what's that?)

Amusing oneself at foreign restaurateurs' attempts at translating the untranslatable is an old game. But the following items, seen on the "English" page of an Avignon café-brasserie's menu in 1981, make the point. Linguists might care to puzzle them out before looking at the French at the foot of the page:

> man toast
> woman toast
> rustic pasty
> growth ham.*

* (Man toast: *Croque Monsieur*, a kind of toasted cheese sandwich. Woman toast: *Croque Madame*, a more luxurious version of the same, usually with a slice of ham. Rustic pasty: *pâté de campagne*, and no relation to a pasty. Growth ham: *jambon cru*, raw ham of the Parma or Bayonne variety — *cru* means raw, but the translator got into a fascinating muddle.)

Hotels

For couples, French hotels are cheaper than British ones. A 60 franc double-bedded room costs 60 francs, whether one or two people sleep in the bed. Naturally, a big room with two double beds costs more than a small room with only one bed; but basically you are paying for the room, not for the number of bodies therein.

Breakfast is normally not included or compulsory, and is of course paid for per head. There are some places, mainly on the Côte d'Azur, which have the breakfast-included (i.e. compulsory) system. The red Michelin guide tells you which hotels these are (once you have mastered the introductory pages). Hotel rooms are good value, compared with Britain; hotel breakfasts not. If you are economising, or just plain mean, you will not take the hotel breakfast; a *café au lait* at a nearby café, and a fresh *croissant* from the *boulangerie*, will be much cheaper. What you would normally get in the hotel would be coffee (or chocolate, or weak tea), a *croissant*, some bread, a pat of factory-wrapped butter and a tiny plastic container of factory-made jam; not a great gastronomic experience, and — at a quarter to a third of what one would pay for a reasonable lunch or dinner in a modest restaurant — distinctly over-priced.

While breakfast is not compulsory, dinner sometimes attempts to be. That is to say, the proprietor will not want you to have his nice cheap room unless you and yours dine beforehand in the hotel restaurant, which may be less nice or less cheap, or both. If you study your Michelin, you will know which hotels follow this practice by the type-face used to indicate the number of rooms in the hotel. If, like us, you are not breakfast-eaters, and when travelling across France have a picnic lunch, compulsory dinner will not be an intolerable stipulation, especially in a country hotel. But if one is making a night-stop in a large town, it is more fun to have a stroll and read all the menus before choosing a restaurant. A few moments planning with the Michelin are indicated.

There is no need to be afraid of hotels in the lowest ("plain but adequate") Michelin category — they are not squalid haunts of verminous characters from the underworld, but clean hotels with at least hot and cold water in every room, though no commissionaire or telly.

There are hundreds of hotels (and villages with hotels and restaurants) not listed in the red Michelin guide. But a proper use of the guide does help to avoid surprises and disappointments.

The number of stars on the plaque by the hotel door has nothing to do with Michelin's stars for restaurants (though it goes to some extent with the number of roofs in Michelin's hotel symbols). These stars convey the offical rating of the hotel for luxury (or simplicity) and therefore price. The prices of the hotel's rooms should also be shown, outside. If not, they are usually clearly on view in the entrance hall or lobby. Embarrassment is thus avoided.

No hotelier will object to showing one the room he is offering. And the price of that room (and of breakfast, and any other extras) should be prominently displayed there.

For some reason lost in the mists of history, the average Frenchman is mean about electric light (much less so about electric heating). The bulb at your bedside will almost certainly be too dim for reading by. Some prudent people who use hotels frequently carry four 60 watt bulbs (110 and 220 volts; screw and bayonet fitting).

No pillow? The normal bed has a bolster *(un traversin)* covered by the sheet. If you don't like this, look in the wardrobe — there may be a pillow (square in shape) there, with extra blankets. If not, ask for one — *un oreiller*.

In ordinary hotels, soap (like toothpaste) is not provided. But a timid request for a tablet of soap *(une savonnette)* might be rewarded, if the shops are closed.

Holiday villas - gîtes ruraux

It is possible to fix oneself up with a holiday villa while in England, through agencies which specialise in this sort of thing, or by replying to advertisements in the papers.

But it is easy enough to find furnished accommodation on the spot, *except in July and August*. The French have long holidays; renting a holiday villa in France is what the average French family likes to do; often Maman and the children will take the accommodation for July and August, while poor Papa, who has only four or five weeks off, will come down when he can.

The demand creates the supply. In country villages, somewhat depopulated as people are lured to towns and factories, a smaller proportions of houses and cottages will be sold off than would be the case in Britain — house property is as good as gold, or better, as a hedge against inflation: a cottage may be kept on for the family's own holidays, and another one may be arranged for letting. Or a village council may buy an empty house and equip it for holiday letting, thus relieving the ratepayer. Often farmers build themselves a new house on the outskirts of their village, having got favourable mortgage terms, and have a self-contained *gîte* built in, thus increasing the value of the property, providing a small extra income, and enabling them to put up friends and relations when the *gîte* isn't let. So there is furnished accommodation available all over rural France (and a lot at the seaside — the more fashionable or crowded, the higher the price). In July and August the French are in it. Outside those months the rent is about half the high season rate, and one can take one's pick.

A GÎTE RURAL is a holiday villa, or flat, or self-contained part of a house, with its own front door, bath- or shower-room, sit-down loo, fridge and all normal furnishing and equipment for holiday letting, which has been inspected, graded and listed by departmental officials, and has had its rent approved as reasonable for its category. It can then wear the "GÎTE RURAL" plaque outside, and be listed (with a brief summary of its features, and its rent at different times of the year) in the official departmental guide to "*gîtes communaux*". A *gîte* France, 178 Piccadilly, London W1V OPQ, will send details on receipt of a stamped addressed envelope. (The French Government Tourist Office is at the same address.) If you are using these lists, do not be put off by the classification "*gîtes communaux*". A *gîte communal* does not imply some sort of communal living. It simply means that the owner of the *gîte* is the *commune*, the council, and it will not necessarily be better or worse than a privately owned one.

From now on, we will use the word *gîte* to mean any rented furnished holiday accommodation, whether or not it is an officially listed *gîte rural*.

So, if you want a *gîte* outside July and August, it is quite practical and sensible to go to one's chosen area, put up at a simple hotel for a night or two, and, armed or not with the official list of *gîtes ruraux*, explore neighbouring villages, perhaps call and enquire at the *mairie*, ask at the village shop... with reasonable luck one will be able to choose among a number of possible *gîtes*. People have turned up in our little village at six, and have found what they wanted before dark. If that fails, call in on an AGENT IMMOBILIER (house agent) — most of them act for land-lords of *gîtes* (but not for listed *gîtes ruraux*). You will expect to pay rather more, as the agent wants his commission (from you or the owner).

Even in July or August one can get fixed up on the spot, but it needs luck and there will be little choice. For those months it is better to book well ahead (in one's previous summer holiday, if one has become addicted to a particular area). The French Government Tourist Office in Piccadilly will help one to make bookings from the list of *gîtes ruraux*. And there are British agencies which specialise in French holiday villas. They often rent a *gîte* from its owner for the whole May-to-September period, and then charge their clients up to twice the normal rent; their profit can be justified (at least from the point of view of the newcomer to *gîte*-renting, especially if he doesn't speak much French) by the fact that they inspect the place themselves, and give a lot of useful information in their catalogues.

Renting from Britons who own places in France, and who advertise them in the British papers, can sometimes be rather expensive, compared with the prices the French charge. Perhaps this is because the British owners are deeply in love with their property and have inflated ideas as to its value; and of course they have to cover the cost of advertising.

In 1980 an average *gîte* for four in a country area in the Languedoc cost around 500 francs a week in July and August, and about 300 in other months.

All one is normally expected to provide for oneself in a *gîte rural* is sheets and towels, though these can often be hired at an extra charge. But unless you want to improvise you will need to bring your tea-pot and kettle, since these are not part of the usual French kitchen. The kitchen will otherwise be well-equipped, as the French take cooking seriously. One's favourite chef's knife deserves its place in the luggage, though.

If you have to deal with an inventory of household items, you will perhaps find the vocabulary on pages 140-143 useful. Names vary in different regions, and some landlords' spelling can be peculiar.

Things to bring
for the store-cupboard

TEA *(le thé)*. One can manage without a tea-pot. But the tea sold in France is horribly expensive. Not only that: its strength and flavour are what might be expected when one reflects that the average native considers it a delicate infusion for the very ill. For a bracing dark-brown tannic brew, strong enough to trot a mouse on or cheer the Eighth Army after El Alamein, bring a good cheap British workers' blend. The French customs are supposed to allow only 100 grams (just under ¼ lb.) per person, but our friends kindly bring us a couple of pounds each time they come and have never been troubled.

KIPPERS.

INSTANT COFFEE *(café soluble)*. We never touch it nowadays, nor does anybody in our very ordinary little village. Nor will you ever be served any in a café or restaurant. Excellent coffee, roasted but not ground *(café en grains)* or ready-ground *(café moulu)* can be bought everywhere, in vacuum packs, and is no dearer than at home. But the instant variety is reputed to be inferior to the British product.

BOTTLED SAUCES. Worcester, H.P., O.K., A.1... the French do not pour bottled sauces on their food. They have mustard, yes, in many delicious varieties, and sometimes tomato ketchup (less vinegary than in Britain, and without much in the way of preservatives, so it may go off after opening). If you have an addict in the family, or if you think your cooking needs it, you will have to go to a big town and seek out an exotic food shop. There, among the smoked elephants' trunks and the tins of chocolate-coated ants, you may find the precious bottle. You will pay appropriately.

MARMALADE *(la confiture d'oranges — la marmelade* can be made of any fruit, or just mean a purée). The "Golden Shred" type can be easily found, but not the chunky kind.

PEANUT BUTTER *(le beurre de cacahuètes)* — another exotic food. We have known Americans suffer terribly from a lack. Can be made for them in a good food mixer: roasted salted peanuts are everywhere, including loose in the market; you just "liquidize" them, perhaps with a little peanut oil *(huile d'arachide,* a common cooking oil) as a lubricant.

HEINZ BAKED BEANS. French canned *haricots à la sauce tomate* are likely to disappoint the juvenile addict.

MARMITE.

BISTO. The late, and greatly lamented, Patrick Campbell lived in Provence, flying regularly to London to record for T.V. He claimed in a *Sunday Times* article that "Madame" used to make him bring back Bisto. We challenged him about this. He admitted that "Madame" had a packet, but it had lasted several years, and what he really brought back was Loch Fyne kippers from Harrods. Well, if you must have Bisto you must bring it with you.

CHEAP FACTORY-MADE CONFECTIONERY — see "Coping with the British Child", page 122. We confess that one of us is always grateful for a dozen bars of Fry's Chocolate Cream.

Some of the above remarks sound snooty. French food is good, and tastes of what it is. "Junk" foods are not so common, and tend to be dearer. Items that would kill the taste of wine are unpopular. For example, a plate of assorted cold meats *(une assiette anglaise,* for some reason) is fine with a red *vin du pays* or something better, but without it, cries out for pickled onions or chutney or piccalilli.

We have racked our brains for items for the section above, which includes all that we have heard visitors lament. Apart from tea, France is not on the whole dearer than Britain once one knows the ropes, and simply abounds in all kinds of delicious things.

One could well bring:
A FEW CHEMISTS' SUNDRIES. Elastoplast *(pansements adhésifs* — rather dear), Dettol, if that is what one is used to, aspirins *(aspirine* — again dearer), Eucryl Tooth Powder... See CHEMISTS, page 88).

Don't over-do it! We have seen people bringing potatoes (better in France, and in greater variety) and even small Camping-Gaz cylinders (made in France).

Presents for the locals

If one lives for more than a few days in a French village, one is liable to put down roots and make friendly relationships. One will soon find oneself receiving small presents, the nature of which will depend on the season and the area, but most probably fruit and vegetables from the proud (and over-productive) gardener. In country districts — certainly where we live — there is a certain amount of etiquette about this, a present calling for a present in return during the next few days. Not that the present-giver will point this out to you! But now that we have a vegetable-garden, and pass on to our village neighbours our surplus tomatoes, beans, aubergines, melons and so forth, we always find that within a short while something is given in return: a few pounds of dessert grapes for instance (for we have no vineyard), or a pot of home-made jam, or even a packet of factory-made sweets. Even a lift in the car to the nearest town is "returned" to us in the shape of some *pâtisserie* bought there. So now, when someone gives us something, we look up our little

notebook to see where we are; and whether we "owe"
anything or are all square.

If one is living in a *gîte* for a few weeks only, one hasn't
got a garden to pick a suitable present from. But a small
packet of inexpensive sweets, for instance, will satisfy
protocol. If when you move into your *gîte* the landlord has
left you some fruit and a bottle or two of local wine, this is
a symbolic return for your renting his *gîte*, so you are all
right. But if you come back to the same place next year,
there is no doubt that you can easily and cheaply win a
reputation for being *gentil* and *sympathique* by bringing a
few trinkets from your native land. We cannot avoid
sounding rather cynical and patronising here: but we are
fairly sure that the most acceptable present for the average
French country-dweller is not the item that would go
down well with the travelled and sophisticated graduate
living in NW3 — the latter goes for the hand-made,
unvarnished, peasanty-looking what-not, but your real
horny-handed peasant, with his rustic background of
colour television and plastic-and-chromium gadgets, feels
that a proper present should be bought, not made, and
come from a large factory, preferably in the Far East. (We
are not of course talking about French intellectuals, who
can give points to Hampstead in the matter of hand-
whittled wooden spoons from the Abruzzi or stone
machins from Macedonia.) So a short visit to Woolworths
in search of chrome ashtrays with Union Jacks on them
and cigarette-boxes exhibiting highlanders will be all in a
good cause. If you can't bring yourself to offer the typical
Taiwan-made souvenir, remember that British sweets are
highly esteemed ("After-Eight Mints" go down well, and
are sold in France at about twice the British price); all
French children and grown-ups have heard of the
Christmas pudding, and small ones come in nicely, with
firm instructions on how long to boil then; and tea-
towels, highly decorated with typical Britons in their
native costumes (Beefeaters, caber-tossers, Prince
Charles...) are received with apparent gratitude.

Fishing

If one has ever been even the feeblest of anglers, it is worth taking some basic equipment to France. There are a lot of rivers, and — despite pollution scares — a lot of fish in them. In the Michelin Camping guide, there is a symbol showing which camp sites are on a river where one can fish. It is pleasant to fish for an hour or so near the tent in the evening, and then leave the rod and line all set up so that at dawn one can pull a pair of trousers over one's pyjamas and try for a trout or two before anyone else is awake.

One really should have a licence. This is not expensive, and can be got at the nearest tackle-and-bait shop; or sometimes a café will be able to issue it. Your *permis* is usually valid only for the *département*, but can be extended for neighbouring ones for an extra fee.

The rivers of France are divided into *première catégorie* and *deuxième catégorie*. In the first, trout predominate, and you may not use *asticots* (maggots) — but cads and bounders can use worms (as is well known, foreigners are cads and bounders anyway). In the second, you can use maggots, and legitimately haul in trout on them, blushing.

The close season (shorter than in Britain), and the minimum permitted size of fish to be landed, will differ from *département* to *département*. Even during the close season, one can be allowed to fish *on Sundays*: your *permis*, or the person who issued it to you, will give details.

No night fishing!

Tackle-and-bait shops abound, where there are good rivers, and of course are good places for advice and gossip. If blue blood runs in your veins, and you have fished only for trout and salmon, you may find a new interest in coarse proletarian angling for catfish in the Loire, and pike are not to be despised. Spinning in the Tarn, you may get three *chevesnes* (chavender or chub) for every trout, but they keep one hopeful.

Shopping

The French again, outside Paris

The great *hypermarchés* and the more modest-sized *supermarchés* offer a painless way (fairly interesting at first, as one compares goods and prices with those at home) of buying some of what one wants. Little need be said about them here, except that they are usually open on Mondays (when most conventional food shops are shut) and stay open quite late in the evening. So they can be handy if one's planning has slipped up. But they don't offer much in the way of human warmth and cheer.

Ordinary shops are more fun. Please don't be in too much of a hurry. The French don't like queueing, but you will usually be reminded when it's your turn. If you know there are half-a-dozen people to be served after you, do not feel you have to rap out your commands quickly, pay up and get out — you might think that this is what the shopkeeper and those waiting would like you to do, but not so. *Bonjour* and *au revoir, messieurs-dames* are the vital minimum to show that you are a member of the human race and acknowledge that the others are too. If you are known at the shop (that is, if you have been there before) the shopkeeper and the other customers would like to know how you are getting on; if you have brought someone shopping with you they want to know his or her relationship to you... Never treat French people as *things*. Satisfy their curiosity. Then buy your items carefully. Even if there are a lot of people waiting, they will be interested as you react to samples of the cheese. If just one slice of ham and one sausage is what you really want, have no fear: these amounts will be served. If you see some enigmatic item on display, do ask what it is. Shopping, especially for food, is a serious business: do not treat it lightly — to do so may save a moment, but shows no respect for the stuff on sale, the people selling it or those looking on and listening in.

This approach — don't be a unit, be a human being, and get on the personal level as soon as possible — can be generalised to wider areas than shopping. French bureaucracy has a fearsome reputation; but if only one can find the person who matters, and become a person to him or her, difficulties melt away. At large post-offices, for example, the officials can be horrid. But at the little one-man post-office we go to, the *receveur* takes a friendly interest in us and our family and our news, looks after our savings account, gives us bits of string to improve our parcels, and money-saving postal advice. Our friendly neighbourhood tax inspector (yes!) helps us fill up our forms and gives us good advice on how to avoid paying anything. We know that if we go to a big garage shortly before closing-time and demand service to our car because they are agents for that make and it isn't closing time yet and we've got the money to pay the employees whose job it is to serve us — we shall get the brush-off. But if we go just after closing time to a small garage and explain what a service they would render us if they would help us on our weary way, we shall very probably be fixed up, and given all sorts of good advice into the bargain; the man and we are reacting at the human level. Liberty, equality and fraternity are not quite empty words. The French are not good at the impersonal doing of duty; they import foreigners to work on the assembly line. If you don't really want to shake hands with ordinary people and at least pretend to take an interest in what makes them tick, avoid rural France — you will save time elsewhere and no doubt get what you pay for. But no more.

Money

Years and years ago the government knocked two noughts

off the franc. Instead of getting 1350 *anciens francs* to the
£, one got 13,50 *nouveaux francs*. But the French have
been slow to respond. If you are asked for a thousand
francs for a pound of pork, don't scream — it's a ten franc
note that's wanted. There's no consistency about this. If
something costs a franc, you will probably be asked for *un
franc*. But if it costs 1,40 F, you might be asked for *cent
quarante* as often as *un franc quarante*. Convenience
sometimes counts, as in house prices, where it is usual to
talk in *millions* — a million old francs, being around a
thousand pounds, is a handy unit for house prices. You
will always be understood if you talk in terms of *nouveaux
francs* — it is after all the official system. And you are
unlikely (since the two systems differ by such a large
factor) to be in any doubt as to what is meant. The only
difficulty can arise in the Midi, where because of the
accent *cent* could be taken by a foreigner to be *cinq*... it is
not unknown, when a *Méridional* (a southerner) has asked
a foreigner for *cent cinquante*, for him to be offered 5,50 F
instead of 1,50 F. One is not likely to be short-changed,
though (except of course in Paris! — where however the
accent problem does not arise).

Prices

Shop cheerfully, shop with care. In France there is a
surprisingly wide price-range for the same article. In big
hypermarchés on the outskirts of large towns, "own brand"
packaged or canned groceries, camping equipment, tran-
sistors, toilet-paper, detergent liquids, and powders,
motoring accessories and so forth are usually cheaper than
in our small town. But other things — fresh vegetables and
morning-gathered oysters, for example — are cheaper and
better than in the *hypermarché*.

How much time one wants to spend comparing goods
and prices is a matter for the individual. No point in
prolonging the shopping when one feels the call of the
beach or the sunlit hill or the shady wood or the trout in

the river. Or work... But if one is settling for a longish period, and above all if avoiding pointless expense means further days or weeks of freedom, it pays — more noticeably in France than in Britain — to do some research on sources of supply.

For long-term settlers, a copy of the big illustrated catalogue of one of the mail-order firms (La Redoute, for example) is useful. Even if one never sends in an order, one gets a good idea of what is available at the lower end of the price range, and learns a lot of vocabulary. (One buys the catalogue at newspaper shops; the cost is refunded on one's first order.)

Markets big and small

Going to the market is perhaps the best way to shop. In small towns or big villages the market may take place once a week, starting about 8 a.m. and ending at 12. If you are going for a short holiday to France, find out quickly when the nearest market is; with luck, a visit should interest the whole family. Merchants of almost everything will have congregated from a wide area, and (apart from the pleasure of wandering around and resisting the STUPENDOUS offers, PRACTICALLY GIVEN AWAY out of the goodness of the salesman's heart to the first ten LUCKY PEOPLE who will believe their good fortune and press NOT A HUNDRED, NOT EIGHTY, NOT EVEN FIFTY, but a mere token forty francs into the kind man's hand) it is a splendid opportunity for the thrifty gourmet to compare quality, price, size and so forth.

In big towns, the market hall is open every day. This will not have the surprises of the once-a-week market, since there are permanent stalls rather than travelling merchants. But it is a most efficient way of doing one's food shopping, since all the fishmongeresses will be in one place, all the poulterers in another, so that comparison is easy. Go fairly early in the morning, before the best is sold (especially for fish). In the red Michelin guide, you will find the permanent market indicated on the town plans by its own symbol.

In villages too small to have a shop, you may meet the travelling merchant. In our village (pop. 100) we have a daily baker; the butcher comes to the square and hoots at 8 on Tuesdays and at 10 on Saturdays (and will bring special orders on Thursdays); and the grocer (and trombonist in the neighbouring town's brass band) hoots *and sings* at about the same times. On Tuesdays it takes them about an hour to deal with the village, on Saturdays twice as long. If you happen to be a holiday-maker staying in the village, these are good times to make yourself discreetly known, and seek advice as to what to buy. There will surely be a dominating old lady *(une maîtresse femme)* to advise you (do not buy those tomatoes — it's only April, so they're unnatural and foreign... or bananas in the summer — God made them to be eaten in the winter when there are no cherries or peaches or melons, and they're too heavy on the stomach for hot weather). It is not a very quick method of shopping, oddly enough — the ladies (who will be going to the weekly market in the town on Wednesdays) buy small quantities of this and that; and a great deal of news and opinion is exchanged. Foreign visitors are welcome at these bi-weekly get-togethers (especially by the grocer, who likes to show off his foreign languages — he has several, restricted however to grocerial vocabulary).

When are they open?

It is always worth bearing in mind that the French start work early, and normally stop at 12 for a couple of hours or longer. The foreigner who adapts to this habit saves himself much frustration (but when driving, 12 to 2 is a good time to get on with it).

FOOD SHOPS may open at 8 or earlier; shut at 12; open again at 2, or 3, or 4, remaining open for 4 hours or more. May be open on Sunday mornings; may be closed all day Monday or just in the morning.

OTHER SHOPS are less likely to open before 8 or to open on Sunday; more likely to be open on Monday afternoon.

SUPERMARKETS, HYPERMARKETS don't usually open on Sunday (though their cafeteria might) but usually open on Monday. Big ones don't shut at mid-day, and may stay open until 10 p.m. or later.

RESTAURANTS do not normally close on Sunday — in fact Sunday lunch is the week's high spot for them (and they may perhaps not serve the cheapest set menu then; the red Michelin guide tells you if this is so, if you have mastered the code in the introductory pages). But they close, normally, on one day a week (not all on the same day in any one town). As you will have guessed, the Michelin guide tells you what day your restaurant closes. If you want to eat at a very popular restaurant in a small town you had better be there by 12.15 at the latest. Dinner starts about 7.30 or 8.

CAFÉS: no general rule. It goes without saying that British licensing hours are regarded with incredulous amazement.

MUSEUMS often shut on Tuesdays.

BANKS: the Financial Times Diary says 9 to 4. But that's only Paris. Round our way it's 8 to 12 and 2 to 5 but it can vary. Normally they're shut on Saturday and Sunday. But in a town near us, where market day is Saturday, they're open then, closing on Monday. The convenience of the customer still counts for a little. It is prudent to note down the hours of a convenient bank as soon as one arrives.

SCHOOLS have Wednesday off, work on Saturday morning.

Food shops

We repeat that France is a land of regional and local variations and traditions. We think that most of what we say is true of most of France; we must apologise to the reader if sometimes we slip up, and dogmatise about a practice which obtains only in the Midi, or only in the Languedoc, or even only in a small area between Montpellier and Béziers.

The baker's - la boulangerie

A shop where bread is sold but not made is a *dépôt de pain*, not a *boulangerie*. Once or twice a day a delicious smell rifts out from the latter, together with people breaking off little samples from their hot loaves.

French bread, though, is not what it was. If one is lucky enough to live near a real small bakery in Britain one may find the French product less good, especially after it's a day old. But *boulangeries* abound; they are never all closed on the same day; no two *boulangers* bake alike. So one can shop around, experimenting, and never having to put up with stale bread.

Names for white loaves are many and various. But the bread is visible in the shop. Point to what you like the look of and say *Un pain comme ça, s'il vous plaît*.

Some bakers make special breads: *pain complet* (wholemeal), *pain de seigle* (rye bread), *pain au son* (bread with added bran). And various rustic-looking loaves *(pain de campagne)*.

They usually sell *croissants* (crescent-shaped pastry-like rolls, for breakfast), the simpler cakes and buns, and oddments depending on the region. We must not generalise. As we keep on saying, France is a land of regional differences and specialities, and French people, including bakers, are individualists.

Wrapped sliced bread can be found in supermarkets. Once in a blue moon someone buys some (to make *croque-monsieur* with: a sort of toasted sandwich). This sort of bread is known as *pain de mie, mie* meaning crumb, as distinct from crust.

The butcher's shop - la boucherie

Strictly speaking, the BOUCHER sells beef, veal, mutton, lamb and usually poultry and game (though you may find a shop specialising in poultry). Pork is the speciality of the CHARCUTIER. But many a butcher's shop is in fact a BOUCHERIE-CHARCUTERIE.

One must forget about the British and American "joint". The animal is cut up differently, along the muscles rather than across them. One result of this is that your meat is largely free of bones and excess fat. Thus, whereas in England — except at very elegant specialised butchers — one finds it difficult to buy a whole fillet of beef, since the butcher does not want to deprive his sirloins of their undercut, in France it is easily obtainable (if one has the money), but one will have difficulty in getting an old-fashioned 10-pound sirloin on the bone.

STEAK: LE BIFTECK is a popular dish. The best cuts have their own names *(filet, contre-filet, faux-filet, rumstek, entrecôte)*. Just *bifteck* comes from a variety of less noble parts of the animal. There need be few problems for the inexperienced shopper, however, since all pieces of meat are (or should be) clearly labelled with name and price per kilo. In the matter of steak you get what you pay for, the cheapest *bifteck* being toughish and stringy but half the price of a nice *entrecôte*.

The English word "mince" has rather depressing associations. Things are better in France, where HACHÉ (except sausage meat) is not supposed to be sold ready-made. Instead, you choose your meat and the butcher minces it for you (often in a superior machine which chops the meat finely rather than squeezing and extruding it). Ask for BIFTECK HACHÉ and you will get fat-free minced beef. This practice means that you can get just what you want; if, for a *farce*, a *terrine* or a *pâté*, you want half a pound of lean minced veal and half a pound of fat minced belly of pork, or a mixture of beef and pork for a hamburger, you can get it. It is always as well to tell the butcher what you want your mince (or other meat) for, as he will then offer the most suitable pieces.

OFFAL (LES ABATS): canny gourmets who know how to prepare such delicacies as brains (CERVELLE, *not* CERVEAU, which is used of the brain in its non-culinary aspect) and calves' sweetbreads (RIS DE VEAU) or the homelier items such as sheep's hearts and pigs' trotters, or have access to such exotica as testicles *(rognons blancs)*, and have been used to getting them almost (or even totally) free in Britain and the U.S.A., will find their purses hurt in France. The French are even cannier gourmets, they know how to prepare these items, and pay the going rate for them. Even pigs' tails have their market (good for pea soup in winter). If you have never gone in for this sort of thing, we strongly advise you, when eating at a restaurant in France, to try TRIPES *(à la mode de Caen*, or *maison*, or any other way), PIED DE PORC GRILLÉ, CERVELLE and RIS DE VEAU in any form. You will probably be converted. Then, when you are back in regions where these things are regarded with suspicion, you will be able to regale yourself and your near and dear deliciously and economically — though your butcher will be unlikely to prepare some items as neatly as in France.

LAMB AND MUTTON: the French, when they come to England, are snooty about which is which (e.g. Tony

Mayer: "*...mouton pieusement baptisé agneau...*"*) — but this is simply a translation trap, since the word AGNEAU refers to a younger animal than the word *lamb*. *Agneau* is strictly speaking AGNEAU DE LAIT, i.e. milkfed, with pale flesh (like veal); MOUTON is red. "Lamb chops" will — unless sweet and tiny — be referred to as CÔTES DE MOUTON; a GIGOT, if it weighs 4 or 5 lb., will be thought of by the English as a "leg of lamb", but the French will think of it as coming from a *mouton*. Use your common sense at the butcher's, and if what you've bought comes from a sizeable animal don't forget to call it *mouton* if you have a French guest. (Don't get inferiority feelings. *Mouton* has a nobler image than "mutton".)

While beef and pork — allowing for the fact that there is less waste with what the French butcher sells you — are not much dearer than at home, mutton and lamb seem very expensive to the British visitor, who appears (1981) to be still profiting by a special relationship with New Zealand. But the French product, in the right region, can be of superb quality (and hard and stringy in the wrong region).

HORSE (CHEVAL): we mention this comestible animal only to point out that your butcher will *not* palm pieces of horse off on his customers, disguised as beef. The horse-butcher has his own special shop which is clearly labelled BOUCHERIE CHEVALINE and usually has a large gilt or red representation of a horse's head above the window. Horse meat is not particularly cheap. *(Bifteck de cheval* sounds odd. But *bifteck* — or *beeftek* or *bifsteack* — means a flat piece of meat for grilling or frying. Beef is *bœuf).*

POULTRY (VOLAILLES): no problems here. One finds a great variety of poultry on sale, even in small towns; all the way from the battery quail to the farmyard turkey. The frozen battery chicken, composed largely of water, is uncommon but can be found. The standard chicken is

* Tony MAYER, *La Vie anglaise*, PUF, 1962.

battery-raised but fresh. However, even in chickens there is great variety, running from the battery chicken to the free-range bird (POULET FERMIER) at nearly twice the price, via the *demi-fermier*, which started life in the battery but had a spell in the open before it met its end.

Brave people buy their chicken on the wing, alive, at the market, and proceed from there. (Proustians will remember Françoise, and her cries of *sale bête* when the lunch refused to die quietly... We have not yet tried conclusions with a determined French fowl.)

If you are having French people in to a meal, present-day chicken, because of the cheapness of the battery product, is not really considered a noble enough dish to invite someone to. Try a guinea-fowl *(pintade)* as a change; it is rather dearer (and thus nobler) than the ordinary chicken. But if you are not used to free-range chickens at home, a real chicken (that is, a *poulet fermier*) can be a revelation. Ideally of course one should get one's poultry from one's *fournisseur* — that nice little farm lost in the hills that makes such a pleasant excursion.

RABBIT (LAPIN), on the other hand, is "noble" enough (and fairly expensive) — perhaps because the French were less affected by myxomatosis or because one does not find cheap frozen rabbit from strange lands in French shops. Wild rabbits are LAPINS DE GARENNE (or warren rabbits) and rabbits raised in hutches are LAPINS D'ÉLEVAGE: quite a different dish.

At poultry shops, do not hesitate to ask for half *(la moitié...)* of a chicken, or half a rabbit, if that is what you would like. Or a quarter *(le quart...)* of a turkey *(une dinde,* or *un dindon)*. They will usually cut it for you.

P.A.C. (usually in the supermarket) means *prêt à cuire* - oven ready. EFFILÉ means that the gut has been removed.

La charcuterie

is where you find most of the things that can be done with
our four-trottered friends. But you find a lot of other
things too: the word *charcuterie* comes from *chair cuite*, or
cooked meat. A very useful place. One of the reasons why
the frozen food section in supermarkets is small, over-
priced and not much used lies in the *charcuterie*: the hard-
pressed working houseperson in search of "convenience
foods" can rustle up a presentable ready-prepared — and
freshly-prepared — meal here quite easily. This fact has
spelt financial ruin to many a hard-up British camper:
resolutions of living simply and frugally on bread, wine,
fruit, sunshine and a little cheese have been known to
crumble at the *charcuterie*, amid the temptations of *pâtés*,
galantines, salami, ham, pies, *rillettes*, ready-mixed salads,
paëllas, little containers of *langoustines à l'armoricaine*,
andouillettes and the day's special *plats du jour*.

It would be pointless to try to list all the things one can
buy at the *charcuterie*, especially because — being family
businesses on the whole — they are all different. And then
there are the regional variations: the beautiful *jambon
persillé*, all pink and green in its jelly, can be got at Beaune
but not at Béziers; where however you can find delicious
little black puddings with pine-nuts and onions in them,
called *morcillas* — not to be found in the Limousin, where
however they make their black puddings *(boudins noirs) à
la châtaigne*, that is with chestnut flour instead of wheat
flour. (The only drawback with that last most seductive of
snacks, if you grill them on your camp-fire, is that inevitably a large posse of dogs with well-conditioned reflexes
will turn up, salivating briskly, from miles around, as
soon as the skin begins to crisp.)

But we can risk a few generalities:

HAM springs first to the Anglo-American mind. The
substance often found in the British "ham sandwich" is
not in fact ham (i.e. JAMBON, the salted and often smoked
leg of the pig) but shoulder: this, known as ÉPAULE CUITE

or ÉPAULE GLACÉE, is a good deal cheaper than any sort of *jambon*. Ask for this, and indeed for any sort of ham, by the slice (so many *tranches*) — and don't be afraid to ask for *une tranche seulement* if this is all you need. Unlike in some countries (e.g. Holland, where the butcher's boy can slide the week-end order under the front door, the meat being in transparent slices apparently cut with a hospital microtome) the slices in France tend to be thickish. So if you want them thin, specify *très mince* (or indeed, in the Midi, *mince-mince-mince*).

JAMBON proper comes in many sorts. The nearest to the universal British ham is usually called *jambon glacé*, *jambon blanc* or *jambon de Paris*. There is nothing special about it. At the other end of the scale are the luxury hams, usually eaten raw *(jambon cru)* as a delicacy (especially by those not afraid of the tape worm, poetically known as *le ver solitaire* — perhaps because one is quite enough). These aspire to the quality of the Italian Parma ham, and some are as good. *Jambon de Bayonne* is best known, but everywhere has its own product, often simply called *jambon de campagne* or *jambon de montagne*. These can be absolutely delicious. If you want to have the best of both worlds, start the day with a pair of fried eggs and a gently warmed slice of the best ham.

BACON: you are unlikely to find anything resembling "best back", that meat being used for other purposes. But "streaky" turns up, called POITRINE SALÉE (unsmoked) and POITRINE FUMÉE (smoked). In general, ham-fanciers are better off in France, bacon-lovers worse off.

SAUSAGES are a vast and fascinating field of study. We must be content with a grossly over-simplified treatment.

First, let us distinguish between the SAUCISSE and the SAUCISSON. A SAUCISSE is flexible, generally soft to the touch and needs cooking, and thus approximates roughly to the British sausage. Only approximately, however, since the *saucisse* is composed of 100 % meat, whereas the British sausage contains a variable proportion of "butcher's rusk". The contents of the *saucisse* (usually called *saucisse fraîche* or *saucisse de Toulouse*) are much more coarsely minced, and look, taste and are much meatier.

The ordinary *saucisse fraîche* is not divided up into four-inch lengths, but is a long tube — so if you want to, you can have a yard-long one. It coils up nicely for grilling.

A SAUCISSON (or more properly a *saucisson sec*) is usually eaten as it is, in thin slices — and of course can be bought by the slice.

It comes in innumerable varieties; any respectable *charcutier* will have a good few of these, so if you want to serve, as an hors d'oeuvre, a selection of *cochonailles* (literally piggybits) don't hesitate to ask for one or two slices of each. Far from thinking you a nuisance, he will be glad to realise that you want to evaluate his wares seriously.

We have already mentioned BOUDINS. You may be disdainful of the British black pudding; and most judges agree that you have every right so to be, since the thing is not what is was in the days of Jude the Obscure and his Arabella (though there are rumours of one or two North-country butchers who make them properly). But do try the *boudin* — in fact try a few. Every *charcutier* makes them differently. Some include onion, some great gobbets of fat, some no fat at all; some currants and/or sultanas, some cream and cognac, and some pine nuts. So they come at all prices. They also come in all the diameters of the pig's gut (and some in his stomach). You will not find all these varieties in any one area. In France one is often surprised at differences in habits and traditions in places only an afternoon's journey away, or less. So, as you wander, try a *boudin* here and there. This advice goes for most other items in the *charcuterie* too. All *boudins* will have been pre-poached, and need only gentle grilling.

If you go in for Chinese cookery, and can manage barbecued spare ribs, you may find the ribs on sale as *croustillou*, or *coustillou*, or *coustillion* or *travers*; the French don't make barbecued spare ribs, Canton style, with them — they just go into cheap stews.

Jane Grigson's Penguin, *Charcuterie and French Pork Cookery* is a splendid book.

Confectionery - *la confiserie*

Confiseurs are often *pâtissiers* as well: éclairs and chocolates at the same shop. If you buy your chocolates hand-made from Charbonnel and Walkers' in Bond Street you may be pleasantly surprised at the prices. Black Magic and Dairy Box addicts, on the other hand, will discover what it costs to make confectionery from egg-yolks, almonds, liqueurs and other nice things. Well worth it, on special occasions — which is when French children get a taste.

Factory-made sweets and chocolates (and bars) can be found at the *épicerie* and the supermarket.

Fish - *le poisson*

All self-respecting markets have fish-stalls, and a fascinating colourful sight they can be. The French buy fish only when it is spanking fresh — or, in the case of shrimps, crabs, eels and often trout, when it is alive. It is a good idea to experiment, instead of sticking to what is sold in England. For example, many Britons have never had a single oyster. At 1981 prices you can buy a dozen oysters (or a kilo, comprising well over a dozen medium sized ones) for less than the price of a British packet of cigarettes, and it would be a pity not to give oneself the

chance of rising to the gastronomic level of Sam Weller or
Dr. Johnson's cat Hodge. And then there is fresh tunny-
fish, the octopus family, and strange creatures for the
bouillabaisse... If you are in the South (and even if you are
not) you should certainly have Alan Davidson's
remarkable and delightful *Mediterranean Seafood*
(Penguin Books — a bargain; there is no French or other
rival at any price). The first half of this 400-page work
lists, with illustrations, almost all the fish you are likely to
see in the market, with general notes on what to do with
them, and their names in most of the Mediterranean
languages (including regional French dialects). The
second half gives recipes, in a practical no-nonsense style,
from all round the Mediterranean. This is one of our
favourite books.

A note on *Lophius piscatorius* (Linnaeus) or *Lophius
budegasa* (Spinola): this important and interesting
specimen, almost unknown in Britain, suffers from well-
meaning translators. It is in the restaurant that you are
most likely to come across it first, as LOTTE or BAUDROIE in
France, *rape* in Spain, *rospo* or *rana pescatrice* in Italy.
Much innocent amusement is caused by restaurateurs'
struggles with it in multilingual menus, especially in
Spain with *rape* (e.g. "rape American style", meaning tail
of this fish *à l'Américaine*); not that the lexical section of
the red Michelin guide to Spanish hotels and restaurants
helps much with its "eel-pout, burbot", which properly
refer to a river fish. There *is* a river fish called *lotte*, to
make matters worse, but in French — at least in the South
— *lotte* and *baudroie* are used interchangeably for the same
sea-fish. Harrap's big New Standard dictionary gives, for
baudroie, "angler(-fish), frog-fish, toad-fish, sea-devil,
fishing-frog", which is a case of *ignotus per ignotum*,
leading to such items as "surprised tail of sea devil" on
the Spanish menu (for the tail, sautéed). The same
dictionary gives, for *lotte*, "burbot, eel-pout", and then
(which Michelin didn't notice) *lotte de mer* as "lophius,
angler". Well... what you do, when you have sampled the

excellent thing called on the French menu *baudroie* or *lotte*, is to ask at the fish-shop or fish market for *queue de baudroie* — only the tail is eaten. Once seen, it is easily recognised. Davidson is good on this. A simple recipe is to poach chunks of the tail (in a *court-bouillon* — see "Cooking with Wine"). When cold, mask them with a mayonnaise-based sauce, and pretend it's lobster.

Fresh sardines and *fresh* anchovies are delicacies not to be missed, if you are anywhere near the sea. And they are among the cheapest fish in the market. They travel very badly — we have seen some fresh sardines on sale in Soho, at a high price, looking much the worse for wear. Do not be like the English family we once met, who — having read of the delights of grilled sardines — were trying to grill some from the tin. See page 116.

Some confusion occurs in cookery books about *morue* — salt cod. *Morue salée* (sometimes confusingly called *morue fraîche*; fresh cod is *cabillaud*, not often seen) is easily identified — it is covered in large crystals of salt, and after being soaked for 24 hours in frequent changes of water, needs very little cooking, and is quite good. Elizabeth David gives *brandade de morue* — there are other recipes, of which we owe the following to that other goddess of the kitchen, Sophia Loren: simply grill nice thick well soaked pieces for a few minutes; serve with a little olive oil warmed with garlic and rosemary. *Morue sèche*, on the other hand, is the stuff you bash against a lamp-post for some time, before soaking it for even longer than *morue salée*, and then cook for ages. It has a strong taste of old cod. You won't find *morue* in Davidson, as it isn't a Mediterranean fish, though much eaten in the area. It may be on sale at the olive-stall rather than in the fish department. Not usually to be found in the summer.

Do not get mixed up about varieties of the octopus family — none of them is a substitute for any other. The squid (ENCORNET or CALMAR) is the one with a transparent "bone", and was created specifically to lend itself to being stuffed with various things — even sausage meat. The cuttlefish (SEICHE) is the one with the white "bone" consumed in Britain by canaries; the skinned body of this is often on sale without the tentacles etc. as *blanc de seiche*. The octopus proper (POULPE) is the tough one, not popular in France — this is the one you see and hear being beaten vigorously against rocks on other Mediterranean shores in a bid to tenderise it. Baby *seiches*, about an inch in size, called SUPIONS, are excellent, but they do take a time to clean; you can sometimes buy them cleaned *(supions nettoyés)*. See page 119. And see Davidson.

Lobsters (HOMARDS) and LANGOUSTES (the claw-less ones, sometimes called in English "crawfish" or "crayfish", leading to confusion with the *écrevisse* or fresh-water crayfish) are just too expensive — and have probably been flown in alive from Ireland, so that millionaires can impress their popsies. The ÉCREVISSE however is much less dear, perhaps because it can be bred in tanks, and is very well worth trying. You buy them alive — reject them if they are dead.

This business of shipping, or flying, shell-fish around is sad for the impecunious gastronome: in the early 1960's we were buying big scallops *(coquilles Saint-Jacques)* in Plymouth market for 3 or 4 old pence each — the locals didn't want to eat them or didn't know how to. Now they get flown around and sell for 25 times the price. (Frogs' legs, by the way, are imported frozen from the People's Republic of China, and Pakistan; and frozen *langouste* from Cuba.)

Unfamiliar shellfish (COQUILLAGES) are best sampled first at a good restaurant — a *plateau de fruits de mer* is a lovely sight, and passes half or three-quarters of an hour most agreeably. Then you can ask the names of the creatures you want to have again (or look them up in

Davidson if you take a copy with you to the restaurant) and note how they have been prepared for you. This may prevent your spending a miserable time trying to do such feats as find your way to the edible part of a sea urchin *(oursin)* by the light of nature, as we once did, having bought a couple of dozen — an experience only rivalled by that of picking the fruit of the prickly pear *(figue de barbarie)* without gloves.

See OYSTERS on page 113.

The grocer's - l'épicerie

The ÉPICERIE has usually turned itself into a small supermarket, and normally stocks:

CANNED FOODS of all kinds (not as popular in France as elsewhere, though some people get fond of French canned peas, which are small and not dyed).

MILK (LE LAIT): there is no "milk round" in France; you will often find fresh milk, but most people use U.H.T. (ultra-heat-treated) milk, sold in plastic bottles or cardboard containers — this keeps indefinitely unopened. "Red" milk (i.e. with a red cap on the bottle) is full-cream, "blue" milk is skimmed. Milk is not considered a *drink* in France, except for small children or as an ingredient in *café au lait*, but glasses of it can usually be obtained at cafés, if one doesn't mind looking eccentric. It won't taste as good as the nice fresh product of the Jersey cow — though perhaps in Normandy one can organise oneself better than in other parts.

CREAM (LA CRÈME): the nearest equivalent to British single cream is *crème stérilisée* in small containers, and is suitable for British recipes. The usual French cream *(crème fraîche)* is matured, and has thickened by natural fermentation, having a very slightly acid, or nutty, taste. If you want to whip this, you may need to add about 1 part of cold milk or iced water to every 3 parts of *crème fraîche*. British cream curdles if you boil it; French *crème fraîche* doesn't, unless you put the lid on — you can use it for thickening sauces, and even reduce them considerably. (Beck, Bertholle and Child, in *Mastering the Art of French Cooking*, who are writing on how to do French cooking in England, say that to make an equivalent of the indispensable French *crème fraîche* you should put a table-spoon of sour cream into ½ pint of British double cream and let it stand for anything from 5 to 36 hours, depending on the temperature, until it has thickened; if you then stir, cover and refrigerate, it will behave like *crème fraîche* — that is, it will keep for 10 days or more and will boil, uncovered, without curdling.) One soon gets to prefer the taste of *crème fraîche*, but disappointment can result if one doesn't know the difference.

The date of expiry *(date limite de vente)* is clearly mark-ed on containers of cream — as with most other perishable products.

CHEESE (LE FROMAGE): there are supposed to be 365 different varieties in France, but this is certainly an under-estimate. Just follow your nose, and let it lead you into interesting experimental nibblings. The French are knowledgeable about cheese. They say that, just as a meal without wine is like a day without sunshine, so a meal without cheese is like a woman with only one eye. This smacks of male chauvinist piggery — why not a man with only one eye? or...?

Outside biggish towns it is as well to stick to fairly local cheeses; if you must have Brie in the Hérault, from 500 miles away, you will find a better sample in Montpellier (200,000 inhabitants) than in the smaller towns. Whether Roquefort is better than Stilton is a debate on which we will not be drawn; but you won't find Stilton outside exotic Parisian shops.

The only imported cheeses the French go in for generally are Dutch (and they make an imitation Edam in Normandy) and gruyère; though what is often referred to loosely as gruyère is in fact Emmenthaler — the one with the big holes — made in France: the usual cooking cheese, for gratins etc. In small and medium towns you won't find Parmesan — a fair substitute is *matured* Dutch Edam (not usually to be found in Britain) called *étuvé* which is fairly hard and grates well enough. The nearest thing to good old mousetrap is *Cantal*.

When you find a cheese that pleases you on the restaurant cheese-board, do not hesitate to ask its name so that you can seek it out when shopping (it will often be a *fromage de chèvre* or *de brebis* — made from goats' or sheep's milk).

YOGHOURT (LE YAOURT): over the last few years the French have taken to this in a big way. (If you are prescribed antibiotics, a French doctor may advise you to take yoghourt twice a day, to help repopulate your intestines with the benevolent bacteria which normally flourish there, but which get knocked out by penicillin etc.) It will be found in many guises: very ecological yoghourt in nice little glass pots, factory-made yoghourt in plastic cups, plain and in all kinds of flavours, and with bits of real fruit in. Some friends of ours make it themselves with little fuss — they put milk and a bit of yesterday's brew in a screw-top glass jar, and take it to bed with them; but it isn't warm enough for the best results.

BUTTER (LE BEURRE) is dearer than in England, because of mysterious E.E.C. goings-on. It is the sign of the Briton to be seen eating bread *and butter* with his meals (butter always accompanies radishes and raw ham; otherwise, except for breakfast, it lives in the kitchen, not the dining-room, since it is thought that there are enough fats in the dishes served). In the northern half of France it is indispensable for cookery; in the South, to make a crude over-generalisation, olive oil is used instead (it's better for you: polyunsaturated!). At big _épiceries_, proper dairy shops and some markets, butter can be bought "loose" from the great mound, and you will be allowed to sample various kinds, for the French can be connoisseurs of butter, and use different types for different purposes. There are many grades and types of factory butter too, pasteurised and unpasteurised. Good French butter is made from matured cream, and has a nuttier taste than butter on sale in Britain. Hence one brand name, NOISY, from the word _noisette_, a hazelnut; our children, when small and camping in France, always loved to have "noisy butter". The same firm also makes a processed emmenthal, which we don't really recommend — who wants _processed_ emmenthal? — unless the idea of _noisy cheese_ sends you. You will have to shop around to find a butter you like.

TEA (LE THÉ): at a price, pale and weak. Bring your own.

MARGARINE (LA MARGARINE, hard g.). Little used, except by the very poor. Cooking oil is favoured for deep and shallow frying.

OIL (L'HUILE, f.): many kinds are stocked in the _épicerie_. The container usually carries a helpful notice saying whether the variety is only for putting on salads etc. _(pour assaisonnement)_ or for frying _(friture_, or _pour frire)_ also; and in the latter case, the temperature it can reach before burning. The most usual oils for cooking are peanut or groundnut oil _(huile d'arachide)_ and sunflower _(huile de tournesol)_. Olive oil _(huile d'olive)_ is dearer, and connoisseurs will have their favourite types — _vierge_ will be the fruitiest. Soya _(soja)_, colza _(colza)_, grape pip _(pépins de raisin)_, walnut _(noix)_ all have their uses. Campers and other people on the move will find that one bottle (chosen for its solidity and means of closure) of _huile d'arachide_ will cover most needs; butter is a greasy nuisance in a proper summer.

La pâtisserie

"Cake" is an Anglo-American concept. *Le cake* means a Dundee-type cake, or dark rich fruit cake, imported from England or imitated in France. The *pâtissier* makes fresh fruit tarts, éclairs, delicious little fattening morsels... Hand-made; expensive by British standards, but then the French don't expect cakes for tea every day. In fact few people, except children, have an afternoon snack, and if they do it is more likely to consist of a roll and a piece of chocolate — just to keep them going until half past seven or eight. The *pâtissier*'s products are more likely to figure as the "pudding" course of a proper meal, especially on Sundays. Sunday morning is the *pâtissier*'s big time: after eleven people like to be seen carrying a carefully wrapped-up cake-box.

Home-made ice-cream is often to be bought here. If made of cream, egg-yolks and real fruit, it will be expensive. Factory-made ice-cream, cheaper, can be got at the supermarket — though again, it will be dearer than the British product, since "non-milk fats" are not allowed. But the usual strange stuff derived from sea-weed and what-not that holds the British concoction together will be included, with enigmatic flavourings and colours. However, like real ice-cream, it is thought of as a luxury, not as an item of daily consumption.

The *pâtissier* will make things to order, writing "Happy Birthday Gladys" on the top. Spell it out for him in capital letters, and get an estimate first.

Vegetables - fruits et légumes

This section is mostly superfluous for the open-minded Londoner. But recently we have been asked by an Englishwoman how to deal with the bundle of asparagus she had been given, and told that the aubergine has never been seen in Aberdeen, nor the courgette in Cardiff. So we include some notes on what is on sale in French markets (not all at the same time of the year). First, however: if you are in a *gîte* in a village, ask if there is anyone who would sell you surplus vegetables. You might get some bargains, and some gossip and local recipes. But vegetables in the market are cheaper and better than in Britain.

The instruction "do not squeeze me till I'm yours" does not apply in France, except for some expensive delicate items. The French housewife chooses carefully. In markets and most fruit and vegetable shops one picks up one of the plastic or metal bowls provided, and puts the items one wants into it. These are then weighed by the merchant.

ARTICHOKES (*artichauts,* m.): Not the Jerusalem artichoke *(topinambour,* m.), which is a tuber, eaten by the French in the 1939-45 war and never again. The *artichaut* is the Globe Artichoke, really a big flower bud. Different sizes and cooking times according to variety. Boil vigorously in plenty of salted water for at least twenty minutes, until some of the "leaves" can be pulled off easily. (Or pressure-cook.) Serve cold, with oil-and-vinegar dressing. Pull off each leaf and suck out the "meat", discarding the rest of the leaf. In the middle you meet the choke — a sort of prickly hay: don't try to eat this. At last you come to the bottom *(le fond)* — the best part. Cans of *fonds d'artichaut* are in the *épicerie.*

ASPARAGUS *(asperges,* f.): There may be a glut in May or June, when it will be cheap. Cut and shave woody parts off the lower part. Tie (twice, for easy lifting) in bundles, and boil in salted water (if you have the right saucepan, you can boil them upright, so that the tender heads just get steamed). Really fresh asparagus takes only about 5 to 10 minutes; otherwise longer. Thick stalks are often tenderer than thin ones. Eat lukewarm, in the fingers, dipping into melted butter.

AUBERGINES (*aubergines*, f.; egg-plant in the U.S.A.): These would be very dull just boiled *à l'anglaise*; but the thing to remember is that they will soak up an awful lot of fat if given the chance. There are innumerable recipes. Our favourite: slice thinly, sprinkle with salt, leave for an hour, wash off the exuded juice, and pat dry. Coat with light batter (one using beaten egg-white is good) and deep- (or wok-) fry. Or put a medium-sized one on a prong and roast it in a gas-flame or an open fire; when it has gone soft, remove most of the charred bits, and mash up the flesh with oil, lemon juice, salt and pepper (a tea-spoonful of sesame oil is nice, with some roasted sesame seeds — not to be found however in rural France); serve as a spread or dip. If you add chopped grilled sweet peppers and yoghourt, you have the Greek *tarato*. Or aubergines can be stuffed and baked — an adaptable vegetable. (See *moussaka* in a good book.)

CELERIAC (*céleri-rave*, m.): Big round roots, seen mainly in the winter. Peel, grate coarsely, blanch for a minute in boiling water, mix with mayonnaise. Serve cold as part of hors d'œuvre. Or very good cut in small cubes and fried; or cut in chunks, boiled with potatoes and mashed together.

CELERY (*céleri*, m.): Usually not as good for eating raw as in Britain. Darker green, it is a cooking vegetable, indispensable for soups and stews; hearts are often boiled and finished off *au gratin*.

CHICORY (*endive*, f.): A splendid linguistic muddle. Chicory is *endive*, endive is *chicorée frisée* (or *scarole*).

COURGETTES, f.: Baby marrows, 3 inches long. Don't peel. Shallow fry, like sausages. At any rate, don't overcook in water. You may be able to get *courgette* flowers — they can be coated with light batter and deep-fried (stuffed or empty).

CUCUMBERS *(concombres*, m.): The short fat rough-looking outdoor ones are good.

FENNEL *(fenouil*, m.): The bulbous swollen base of the stems can be thinly sliced and eaten raw. We find this delicious; but some people don't like the mild aniseed flavour. Older or tougher specimens should be boiled until tender, sliced in half and finished off *au gratin*.

Feathery fennel fronds are often used as a flavouring for fish (in the *court-bouillon* — see page 106 — or inside and around the fish as it grills). But you won't find such fronds on sale. They come from the wild fennel plant, seen growing at the roadside.

FUNGI: The *champignon de Paris* (m.) is the ordinary British mushroom; cultivated, can be bought at any time. For stews, *vol-au-vents* etc., canned ones are convenient and obtainable everywhere.

The CHANTERELLE (f.) or GIROLLE (f.) (cantharellus cibarius) and the CÈPE (m.) (boletus edulis) are mor highly prized; they are gathered wild, and so appear i. the market only sporadically. Not so good in tins. To experiment, clean very well and cook gently in a little oil. Dried *cèpes* are sold in little packets; soak in tepid water, then add to stews.

LETTUCE: this is mentioned because: (1) although the French for lettuce is *laitue* (f.), *salade* or *salade verte* means plain lettuce with oil and vinegar dressing. Anything incorporating bits of apple, shrimps or what-not is a *salade composée*; (2) in the South you will see rather dim-looking small lettuces on sale, of the variety *sucrine*, which are in fact good, full of heart, and crisp; (3) if you are entertaining French people, they will be grievously disappointed if they don't get a little *salade verte* after their meat course. When lettuce is unobtainable, endive *(chicorée frisée* or *scarole)* may be substituted.

ONIONS: Mentioned because you can get large, very mild onions for eating raw in salads (*oignons doux*, m., known down our way as *cèbes*, f.). We gave a couple one morning to a gentleman from Lancashire: he took a small slice very suspiciously, and then polished them off as though they were peaches. They weighed a pound each. He was all the better for them, and became an addict. They don't keep, so you can't always get them.

PEAS - THE ONES YOU EAT POD AND ALL (*pois mangetout*, m.): Much better known in France than in Britain. Delicious. Top and tail, string if necessary; boil for a very short time, serve with melted butter.

QUINCES (*coings*, m.): They look like large roundish pears, but must not be mistaken for such. Make jam with them; incorporate thin slices with stewed apple, apple pie, etc.

SWEET CORN (*maïs sucré*, m.): Not to be found in the shops, except canned, in the exotic foods section. What you see growing is maize.

SWEDES (*rutabagas*, m.): Only in the war (see Jerusalem artichokes, *topinambours*, above).

SWEET PEPPERS (*poivrons*, m., or *poivrons doux*): Cut in half, remove seeds, slice thinly and eat raw with *oignons doux* and tomatoes. Or stuff and bake (well-flavoured cooked rice is a good stuffing base). Or make *ratatouille* — a mixture of sweet peppers, courgettes, aubergines and tomatoes, with garlic and herbs, stewed in their own juice with olive oil.

TOMATOES (*tomates*, f.): Ugly ones are nicer — unless you are a wholesaler interested in transporting thick-skinned shock-proof ones, uniformly round and red, to sell to people who buy with their eyes only. Go for big irregularly shaped varieties, very popular in France, especially in the South.

Other shops

The bookshop - la librairie

For a few years retail price maintenance was abolished in the French book trade — unlike in Britain. This meant that bestsellers, such as the Michelin guides, cost less in the rudimentary book sections of big supermarkets than in proper bookshops. This was hard luck for good booksellers, who otherwise would expect sales of such fast-moving items to subsidise the valuable service of stocking less popular works. But as from 1982 that has been changed. One will no longer save money by buying books at the *grandes surfaces*. Please encourage the small bookseller!

THE LIBRARY *(la bibliothèque)*: Only in big towns will you find a proper library, with space to work in.

The chemist's - la pharmacie

La pharmacie stocks medicines. It will also have some "beauty products" (though these will be found in profusion at *la parfumerie*), a few of the more expensive kinds of toilet article (soap and so forth can be got at a *droguerie* or supermarket) and sanitary towels. It does *not* stock: photographic equipment; films; gramophone records; cassettes; stationery; picture postcards; home wine-making equipment; dog brushes; toys; Christmas decorations... It is, in short, not Boots.

The *pharmacien* is a qualified dispensing chemist and first-aid expert, who must by law own and be responsible for his shop. He is allowed a good profit margin (medicines cost more than in Britain), and especially in country districts is regarded as the first person the sick or injured consult. Go to a *pharmacie* in the first instance, if you should suffer from minor accident or malaise; if you really need a doctor, the *pharmacien* will without hesitation point this out, and tell you where to find one. And he will usually be glad to identify the mushrooms you have gathered.

ANTISEPTICS (ANTISEPTIQUES, M.): the usual ones are 90° alcohol *(alcool à quatre-vingt-dix degrés)*; or ether *(éther, m.)*; or hydrogen peroxide *(eau oxygénée, f.)*. On minor grazes, after cleaning, *mercurochrome (m.)* is often used. This is a bright red dye, producing a spectacular effect on small boys' knees.

ASPIRINS: COMPRIMÉS (M.) D'ASPIRINE (F.).

COTTON WOOL (LE COTON HYDROPHILE). Also at the supermarket. (Old dictionaries sometimes give *ouate*; as far as we can discover, this is a substance used for cleaning steam engines.)

DISPOSABLE NAPPIES (COUCHES, F.). Bags of a dozen or more. Also at the supermarket.

ELASTOPLAST. Ask for *pansements adhésifs (m.)*.

OINTMENT is *pommade (f.)*.

PILLS, TABLETS are *comprimés (m.)*.

SANITARY TOWELS are *serviettes hygiéniques* or *serviettes périodiques (f.)*. Also at the supermarket. Tampax are Tampax.

ÉLIXIR PARÉGORIQUE (M.) is the traditional remedy for "holiday diarrhoea". Opium-based and aniseed-flavoured, it is sold only in small quantities, and tastes rather like

Pernod. It often works. It corresponds to the good old kaolin-and-morphine mixture, without the kaolin.

PRÉSERVATIFS (M.), contraceptive sheaths, are sold by the chemist.

NOTE: 90° alcohol as sold by the chemist is perfectly drinkable if diluted to half strength (thus bringing it to about the strength that gin, vodka, etc. is sold at). Many people use it to make liqueurs. This is illegal, but solely because drinks are much more highly taxed: instead of using alcohol from the chemist at about 20 francs the litre and breaking it down with water to make two litres, they are supposed to buy *alcool blanc pour fruits*, at 45° and at over 40 francs the litre... This is why the chemist, unless he knows you as a steady reliable person not given to public displays of drunkenness, will not sell you more than $\frac{1}{4}$ litre at a time. We know English people who take it home at full strength, breaking it down later. From the point of view of the British customs officers, alcohol is alcohol, whether it's 90° or 30°, for one's duty-free allowance.

Beware of experiments, however! *Alcool modifié* is also sold by the chemist, and this is not for human consumption; nor is *alcool à brûler*, the equivalent of methylated spirits, on sale at the *droguerie*. It is best to put one's cards on the table and ask the chemist *"Est-ce qu'on peut en faire des liqueurs?"* (Can one make liqueurs with it?)

The ironmonger's

Two shops: LA QUINCAILLERIE and LA DROGUERIE.

The dictionary suggests that *le quincailler* is the iron-monger. But he mongs only iron, and metallic objects: tools, power drills, screws, nails, folding grid-irons...

La droguerie does not stock drugs or medicines, but has most of the non-metallic things you get at a British ironmonger's: brushes and brooms, door-mats, detergents, fertilisers, furniture polish, weed-killers, paint, plastic bowls, *jerricans* for the wine from the *cave coopérative*, corks, moth-balls, insecticide... and some of the non-medical things you get from the chemist in Britain: soap, both household *(le savon)* and toilet *(la savonnette)*, hair-pins, nail-scissors...

We are not attempting a vocabulary. Most items are vis-ible; for the rest, if a pocket dictionary, our inventory on pages140-143, and the essential technical words on page 24 fail, there may be (infuriating assertion) "no demand for it".

The laundry - la blanchisserie

First, the good news. If you are in a *gîte* you may find that your village has a *lavoir*, where for centuries the inhab-itants have done their washing. In our village it is near the spring. The water feels cool in summer, but in winter one notices that geology has taken the chill off. The village ladies all have washing machines, but they are convinced that there is nothing like a good rinse in half a cubic metre of spring water. Nowadays it flows into half a dozen big troughs, and one never has to wait to find one free. If you can stand the thought of doing the smalls in cold water in the open air, this is fine; and you can have a good gossip with the locals. Just by the *lavoir* are the village washing lines. Wash before breakfast, dry by eleven, during *la belle saison*. A sheet was stolen — the scandal is still discussed. It happened in 1956...

The *lavoir* is free, and you don't have to ask anyone's permission.

Now the bad news. Perhaps because almost everyone has a washing machine (and in France there are some quite cheap small plastic ones on the market) washeterias (laundrettes) are few and far between. Ask at the *syndicat d'initiative* where the nearest *blanchisserie automatique* may be found, and don't be surprised if it's forty miles away.

There are however small laundries *(blanchisseries)*. These tend to take several days over your order, and are relatively dear. But the job is usually beautifully done, whether it's sheets or real silk blouses.

The post office, stamps, telephoning: les P. T. T.

Large French post offices are nasty, small ones are nice. You *can* make friends with the ladies in the large ones, but you are more likely to be immediately regarded as an interesting human being in the small ones.

The holiday-maker is unlikely to need to go to a post office, except to get an up-to-date list of postal charges or have a letter or package weighed. You can buy stamps at any *tabac* — the shop licensed to sell cigarettes, with its "carrot" sign outside. The tobacconist cannot be relied upon, however, to be up-to-date in postal rates for foreign countries.

Up to a few years ago, France had the worst telephone system of any civilised country. One used to make telephone calls from cafés, or from post offices if one wanted to phone abroad; and there were hair-raising complications, frustrations and delays. It is unreliably rumoured that this was the fault of de Gaulle, a highly literate man who wanted to encourage the French to write, and refused to allow the telephone system to be properly developed. If that was the case, Giscard d'Estaing abandoned the attempt — the French still write letters with extreme reluctance, owing to their traumatic struggles with the nitty-gritty of written French grammar

at school, but they now have a good telephone system.
And almost every village has a spick-and-span new
telephone kiosk, from which you can dial direct to most
European countries and the United States. Instructions
are displayed in several languages including English (and
the British Post Office issues a leaflet on telephoning to
Britain from Europe).

The latest type looks like a shiny modern gambling
machine. You start by putting in coins, which remain
visible in glass-fronted slides; and when you have been
connected to the number you are calling, the coins start
disappearing one by one as the minutes — or the seconds
if you are phoning abroad — tick away. You can top them
up as the call proceeds; a light begins to wink when you
risk being cut off. As you hang up, the surplus coins are
returned to you. If it doesn't work, and retains your
money, go and complain vigorously at the nearest post
office — they are allowed to make a refund if you seem
honest (and have proof of your identity).

The tobacconist's - le bureau de tabac

Postage stamps *(timbres-poste, m.)* can be bought at the
bureau de tabac (usually called *le tabac*). Don't queue for
them at the post office. *Le tabac* is often the newsagent's,
selling postcards and other oddments; or may be com-
bined with a café. You can also buy your car tax sticker
there *(la vignette)* if you are a settler.

Cigarettes: some are imported brands, almost as
expensive as in Britain; some French-made ones imitate
these, being made of Virginia-type tobacco *(tabac blond).*
Others are made of dark tobacco *(tabac noir).* The most
popular of these, and the cheapest, are *Gauloises.* Many
people prefer them with filter tips *(Gauloises filtres)* as
otherwise little bits of loose tobacco keep coming out.

However beautiful your French may be, you will be at once recognised as a foreigner if you ask for *"vingt Gauloises"* (or *twenty* of any other brand) — ask for *un paquet de...*, since they all come in packets of twenty.

French cigars are cheaper than imported ones. *Voltigeurs* are traditional: strong black stuff.

Wine - le vin

We shall not try to describe the great clarets and noble burgundies. There are plenty of books on the subject, ranging from fairly practical wine atlases to gushing examples of *belles-lettres*. Wine arouses the sun-starved Anglo-Saxon muse. If you are a wealthy connoisseur, equip your Rolls-Royce with a shelf full of guides to the best vineyards, where each grape is lovingly picked at the right hour of the right day by the seventh son of a seventh son, and have a lovely tour.

Oddly enough, if your income is more modest, and you like a really good bottle of *vin fin* once a month or so, you are better off in London — or even Blackpool. The strange effects of excise duty on the volume of wine instead of on the value, and of V.A.T. (and T.V.A., its French equivalent) and the economics of the wine trade, is that on the whole if you want to pay a lot for a bottle (say £5 or more) you will get a better wine in Britain than in France. And reliable British wine merchants have centuries of experience. You are doomed to disappointment if you expect to drink a daily magnum of first-growth claret at half-price in France.

But France is also the home of very cheap decent ordinary wine. No need to drink it kneeling; good healthy stuff to be grateful for at every meal of the day without having to worry about the cost. At the moment we have as our daily wine a nice *vin du pays* which we collect from the producer at just over 3 francs the litre. The normal wine-bottle is 75 cl, so at 11 francs to the £ our wine costs us about 20 p. the bottle; and this is not the cheapest good wine one can find. This makes a wonderful difference to the life of the improverished intelligentsia. Cook with it!

Put ice-cubes in it on a hot day if you want to! Don't *fuss**
about it!

Buying your wine is rather less easy (and more interesting) than in England. You will search in vain for something like a fine old-fashioned British wine merchant's
shop, with its fascinating list of vintages and dignified
gentlemanly assistants; or for the more modern wine-shop
with its brightly labelled bottles from all over the globe.
In fact you probably won't find a wine-shop at all. In the
matter of fine wines and daily wines (as in the matter of
chickens, eggs, hams and other items) the able Frenchman
has his *fournisseurs* — that is, he buys at the source (or
pretends to). You will find in the small grocery, ordinary
supermarket or mighty *hypermarché* a modest but not
stunning selection of wines, from champagne (which
everyone needs from time to time) down to ordinary stuff
sold in plastic containers or in glass litre bottles. (With the
last, don't forget that there is money on the bottle. If it's
the standard litre bottle you can take it back to any shop.
But it's worth while hanging on to a half-dozen or so
empty bottles, as we shall see.)

It is better, cheaper and more fun to have your own
fournisseur. And — assuming you are in a wine-producing
area — there's not much difficulty about finding one. As
you drive around you will see signboards: CAVE
COOPÉRATIVE DE X or DOMAINE DE Y offering *dégustation
gratuite* and *vente de vin* (free tasting! wine for sale!).
Depending on the size and pretensions of the
establishment, you may be offered a tour of the vats, the
bottling machinery etc. What you are interested in is not

---

* Pamela Vandyke Price, in *The Times* of April 11 1981, says that when
squeezing a lemon on one's fish one should *be sure to do it with the left
hand only — otherwise the drinker will find that the stem of the wine glass
smells so strongly of lemon that the wine's bouquet has to battle to be
noticed.* Well, yes. Good girl, Pamela. Personally, we are pretty ambi-
dextrous with the wine glass, and any normal butler (who will of course
have given the stems a precautionary sniff before announcing dinner)
will beckon one of the footmen whenever a squeeze is required. But it's
nice to know how they manage in Balham.

wine in bottle, but *en vrac* (on draught: literally, loose).
Very elegant concerns may not sell it like that, especially
if they produce only *appellation contrôlée* or V.D.Q.S.;
having done some free *dégustation* of their range, you
might as well take away a bottle or two of what takes your
fancy. If — as most places do in the Midi — they sell *en
vrac* this is much more economical, because in the case of
ordinary wine the cost of bottling etc. doubles the price of
the product.

Now you need something to take away your wine in.
The most picturesque is of course the big spherical heavy
glass *bonbonne* in its wicker (or plastic) cover, holding
anything from five to thirty litres. Although this looks
nice, we do not recommend it. Not just because it is
rather dear, but because it is less practical than the
alternatives (though better for storing wine in for long
periods). There is a lot to be said for the five-litre *jerrican*
in *plastique alimentaire*, costing about 12 francs. This is
light (unlike the *bonbonne*) and has a useful spout. It is not
for long-term storage. It is a sensible thing always to have
a couple of these in the car; if you are going anywher
new, you can pop in to any interesting *cave* you come
across, have a chat and a bit of *dégustation*, and take away
five or ten litres at two or three francs the litre.

But you will have to bottle it. Wine will not keep for
more than a day or two once you have left a lot of air in its
container. This is where your small collection of empties
comes in handy. By all means pour straight from jerrican
to wine-glass if you are a large party and are going to get
through that jerrican at one meal, or at any rate in one day
(though without being wine-snobs we prefer to decant it).
Buy conical corks *(bouchons coniques,* m.) at the *droguerie,*
not cylindrical ones — the latter are better if you want to
lay the stuff down for a few years, but you need a special
device for getting them in, whereas a conical cork goes in
with a blow from a hammer or (better) a chunk of wood.
Bottle it when you've brought it to your temporary home,
and then you've got your couple of jerricans empty, ready
for the next excursion.

Another solution is the *cubitainer* (one of Britain's exports, oddly enough). This is a plastic cube, with a proper little tap, in a protective cardboard box. The great thing is that you do not need to let air in to get the wine out. The plastic collapses round the wine as it is drawn off, all but the last two or three litres. When you get down to these, either the wine won't come out unless you tilt the cubitainer to let air in through the tap, or you hear air being sucked in without your having to tilt; drink those last few litres quickly, or bottle them. So the bottling chore is (largely) eliminated. The cost is not much — between a franc and 2 francs per litre capacity, according to where you buy your cubitainer. A lot of *caves* will sell you the cubitainer at cost. You can get them in various sizes. We prefer the smaller ones, around 10 litres. Larger sizes can be hard to hump about; 30 litres of wine, even in a light cubitainer (or plastic jerrican) weighs 30 kilograms, or over half a hundedweight. Cubitainers are not supposed to last for ever. But we kept a 10-litre one going (for daily drinking, refilled from bigger jerricans) for over two years before it sprang a leak.

Jerricans or cubitainers are practical for taking wine home to Britain in. A dozen normal (75 cl.) bottles makes a bulky package for only 9 litres, but a cubic foot contains 28 litres, and 9 litres would fit into a 9-inch cube. Plastic is lighter than glass, too.

At present (1981) the British Customs allow you to bring home duty-free 7 litres of table wine per adult head, if you don't also bring other alcoholic drink such as spirits and if the wine was bought in the E.E.C. Above 7 litres (or 4, if you have spirits) you pay rather more than £1 per litre. Even so, a couple we know take home every year 80 litres of our local 3-franc wine, paying the duty on 66 litres, and find it a bargain.

When you buy your wine *en vrac* you will be asked where you are going with it, how long you will take on the journey, and what is your car number. A pink form will then be filled in for you, giving all these details, down to the time you are starting out from the *cave*. Don't be intimidated by this. It is meant to identify wine being transported in bulk, and anyone transporting bulk wine, whether it's 10 litres or 10,000, has to have one of these pink forms with him on his journey. No policeman or inspector has ever stopped our car to see if we've got bulk wine on board; it needn't interfere with your plans: if it's early in the morning you can still go for a long joy-ride with your wine, as long as some indication of your itinerary and destination is put on the form. It will make life difficult for you only if you have been fortunate enough to inherit a nice little château in the best part of the Bordeaux area, and think it would be a good idea to stretch your output by mixing in a few hundred thousand litres of our good Midi wine (the operation can be achieved — there was a big claret scandal some years ago).

The best way of assessing the quality of a wine is to drink it. With due respect to philosophers from Plato to Karl Popper, it can be held that if you like it, it's Good; at any rate as far as wine is concerned. But there is a certain amount of official nomenclature which is not wholly meaningless:

A.O.C. *(appellation d'origine contrôlée).* This is the product of a certain vineyard, or a certain district, or a certain *commune*, and in each case certain stringent regulations are laid down. These concern the variety (or varieties) of grape used, the method of pruning the vines, the use of fertilizers, the method of making the wine and maturing it, and the maximum yield (any surplus being sold under a more modest label). The regulations for each wine are laid down very precisely, and have to be equally precisely observed. This is not dictation from above so much as agreement among local growers to maintain the quality and fame of their product; a scandal which outrages local chauvinism results from any transgression discovered by the powerful inspectorate.

V.D.Q.S. *(vin délimité de qualité supérieure).* The regulations are similar to those for A.O.C. but less stringent; for example, more highly productive but less "noble" varieties of grape may be used, in proportions laid down for each wine. There is strict analytic control, and (unlike the A.O.C.) the wine has to be passed by a tasting committee of experts. (As many of these wines may be struggling to get into the A.O.C. class, they can represent very good value).

VIN DE PAYS: This will be a wine from one defined area, i.e. unblended; made from approved varieties of grape, and subject to organic analysis and tasting tests.

VIN DE TABLE: otherwise *vin ordinaire* or plonk. This can be the result of blending, and is often sold under a brand name, and always with a mention of its alcoholic strength (usually 9°, 10°, 11° or 12°). Cheap, but not at all to be despised; you may well find that a local *cave coopérative* produces a wine of this sort which, for everyday drinking, pleases you as well as, or more than, a nearby V.D.Q.S.

VIN DOUX NATURELS — V.D.N. — AND VINS DE LIQUEUR are wines where the fermentation has been stopped by the addition of alcohol, producing a strong and (usually) sweet wine. Nice with strawberries.

FIZZY WINE: VIN MOUSSEUX. A bottle of good champagne costs almost as much in France as in Britain; but in France a dozen bottles of the cheapest sparkling wine can be bought for the price of a bottle of Veuve Cliquot. Indeed, in France a really good bottle of sparkling cider (it can be excellent) costs more than a cheap sparkling wine. What with taxes and transport costs, inferior sparkling wine is over-priced in Britain, by the champagne standard. But in France, a 6-franc bottle of *vin mousseux*, made by the economical *cuve close* method instead of the *méthode champenoise*, has its uses. At about three times that price you can find some nice non-champagne wines made by the *méthode champenoise* — the difference, to the drinker, is that the bubbles last longer; but as the finished product is bound to cost more, a better basic wine is likely to be used.

The cheapest *mousseux* is fun, with, say, a little

pâtisserie. Children love it! And why should one grudge them this exotic pleasure? The wine has a low alcoholic content. And the bottle looks and behaves just like a champagne bottle. The *sommelier* in a good restaurant knows how to remove the cork from a bottle of champagne without projecting it across the room with a bang or wasting a drop: but one of our pleasantest memories of camping in France is of the joy of our little son, as he managed to shoot a cork right across the river, before pouring out all round and settling down to his fresh strawberry tart with "champagne". One isn't always on holiday...

Holiday Cookery,
mainly for campers

We include a section on cookery with trepidation and humility. The shelves of British bookshops and of British kitchens groan under the weight of beautiful or plain-and-practical cook-books. Some people seem to read gastrography as others read pornography; the business is booming. Take your favourite books; don't leave Elizabeth David behind; find room for Jane Grigson.

All we aim to do here is to suggest a few ideas for enjoying things that are good and comparatively cheap in France, and which can be cooked even in reduced circumstances — on a camp-site, for instance, with only one gas-ring, or in a *gîte* without the gadgets (and probably without the oven) that one has at home. (See also the notes on vegetables starting on page 83.)

We have spent several six-week camping holidays in France, with our tent, our sleeping and cooking gear and our two grown-up-sized children, all in and on a Volkswagen Beetle. Unless you have much more room than we had, we would advise you to be content with the small one-cooking-ring Camping-Gaz cooker. Two-ring ones, with large gas-cylinders, are disproportionately bulky, and a lot can be done with one cooking-ring. On the camp-site one sees the typical French family, settled for a month or more, with elaborately equipped kitchen tables, and charcoal barbecues with electrically driven spits — and *Maman* making the winter's supply of jam from cheap local peaches when she isn't creating traditional dinners. Well, we were first up Everest.

Apart from the cooker, we advise:

- a good frying-pan, large and heavy, not a flimsy "camper's" affair;

- a pressure-cooker (not just for pressure-cooking; since it has a firmly-fixed lid, if you use it as an ordinary saucepan you can knock it over without disaster to food or feet; and when travelling it acts as a good storage-place for opened packets etc.);

- a soup ladle (for getting soups and stews out of the pressure cooker, especially if it is the sort whose sides curve in at the top);

- a small kettle (it won't matter if it is light and flimsy if it is the whistling sort which you fill through the wide spout; this spills less hot water when knocked over);

- a French collapsible wire salad-basket (not just for whirling salads around in to dry them, but also as a hanging vegetable rack in the tent);

- an asbestos mat, for gentle stewing;

- insulated beakers;

- unbreakable clear glasses for wine (one can drink wine out of anything; but it aids to the pleasure if one can see it in the glass);

- whatever common-sense dictates, in the matter of plates, bowls, knives, forks, spoons etc.; we plead for steak-tongs, a fried-egg lifter, an oyster-knife and some good sharp cook's knives, of a size that allows them to be used as table-knives — it spoils one's enjoyment of a well-flavoured but slightly tough steak if one has to wrestle with a flimsy blunt "camping" knife; but plastic plates and bowls will do;

- a plastic bucket, preferably the square kind; for carrying washing-up in, and other things; and for packing things in when travelling;

- an insulated food-box, at least big enough to hold a few bottles of white and rosé wine, and litre beer and lemonade bottles, with one of those "thermic packs" that you can get refrozen at the shop in big camp-sites (ice can also be bought here and there);

- and we make a special plea for a good large thermos

flask. This not so much for keeping drinks hot in, as for a number of one-burner cooking dodges. For example, you want to serve steak or sausages, with Instant Mash (the latter being well tolerated by the young — see Coping with the British Child, page 122). Before you start cooking the steak or whatever, put the required amount of potato powder in a bowl, and the required amount of water in the kettle. When it boils, pour it into the thermos, where it will remain for ages at the right temperature to be poured on to the potato for *really* instant mash that hasn't got cold waiting. Other stratagems, with soups and so on, will suggest themselves; the point being that with one-burner cooking it is useful to be able to produce instantaneously a pint or more of near-boiling water.

Instant Mash is not an inspiring subject, and we would prefer fresh French bread as "padding". But it is a good example of one-burner technique. Similarly, boiled potatoes are out — they monopolise the little burner for far too long, what with boiling the water first and then boiling the potatoes. So are proper (not tinned) spaghetti and other pastas: they need too much boiling water; and disaster results if you try to boil spaghetti in too little water — a soggy sticky mass. But couscous, as a filling alternative, demands only the amount of boiling water that it will absorb (see page 108). And see RICE, page 108.

Your camp-site may allow you to build twig or charcoal fires for grilling, or there may be a big communal one. So a folding wire grill, bought in France, will be useful (see Grilled Fresh Sardines, page 116).

If you are going to a *gîte* you may (and certainly should, if the *gîte* has been equipped for French people) find almost all you need for cooking. But it is wise, if you want tea, to bring tea-pot, kettle, tea-strainer, and indeed tea. You may want your favourite cook's knife; and perhaps your own tin-opener. You will, by the way, almost certainly be cooking on gas, from cylinders.

Cooking with wine

Very gentle (below boiling-point) simmering in wine or wine and water is an absolutely basic cooking method, neglected in Britain for obvious reasons. In France there is fortunately no need to skip, with a sigh, a recipe as soon as it says "add half a bottle of dry white wine". It is not only a question of flavour; wine makes meat more tender. (There should, by the way, be no alcohol in the finished product — it vapourises early in the proceedings). If you have facilities and time, you should use the recipes of the goddesses of the kitchen mentioned on page 17. The first three recipes below, however, will show what wine can do.

Simple beef

You could call this *bœuf bourguignon*, but that is really more complicated (the best recipe is in Beck, Bertholle and Child).

Equipment: one saucepan (ordinary; or enamelled cast-iron casserole, etc.; but not naked cast-iron or the colour of the stew will be affected); one gas-ring.

Ingredients: stewing beef (ask for *bœuf bourguignon*), red wine (Elizabeth David rightly says the better the wine, the better the dish. Made with a good burgundy, this dish will be 15 times better than if you used water; made with cheap local wine, it will be only 10 times better); a big onion, a little garlic and two or three carrots (desirable but not essential); flour, oil, salt, pepper, perhaps a squeeze of tomato purée from a tube.

Roll bite-sized chunks of beef in seasoned flour. Chop onion and carrots, and gild them in a little oil in the saucepan. Remove them (or not, if in a hurry — but removing them enables you to get the oil hotter), adding a little oil if necessary, and brown the beef. Put the onion and carrot back with the beef, add a little chopped garlic, and red wine to come two-thirds of the way up. Bring to a

boil, and stir. Then turn the heat down, cover, and cook
below boiling point until the beef is tender — or as tender
as you think it will ever be. An hour is a minimum. At any
point you can remove the saucepan and start again later
on (e.g. if you've only one burner, and want to get on with
something else). Taste, and correct seasoning. The colour
can be improved by adding a little tomato purée. Have no
inhibitions about adding things at a suitable time —
mushrooms (fresh or canned — there are plenty of the
latter on the shelves of the *épicerie*); a few stoned black
olives, bits of unsmoked bacon; some *couenne* (see page 74)
could well have gone in when you added the wine — to be
removed before serving. But if all one can lay one's hands
on is beef, wine, salt, pepper and a loaf of bread — and
some more wine to drink — one can survive.

Poached fish

Equipment: one saucepan (or deep frying-pan, to be
covered with aluminium foil); one gas-ring.

Ingredients: fish — a nice piece of turbot, or a sole, or
some rolled-up fillets of sole — or, less expensive than
these, any firm-fleshed white fish. It or they should fit
fairly neatly into your pan. In a really well equipped *gîte*
there might, with luck, be a long fish-kettle, with grid for
getting the fish out without damaging it; or even a
turbotière; *court-bouillon* to cover fish.

You make your *court-bouillon* by taking roughly equal
parts of water and dry white wine, adding a touch of wine
vinegar, and simmering for half-an-hour with herbs and
other aromatic ingredients: chopped onion or shallot,
sliced carrot, a bay leaf, some celery leaves, thyme,
parsley, fennel, peppercorns — all or some. A short walk
might find the bay *(laurier-sauce)*, thyme and fennel
(fenouil); a request for *des fines herbes pour un bouquet
garni* or *pour faire un court-bouillon* at the market should
do the trick. Then poach — *don't boil* — your fish in it

until done. You then remove the fish and, if you wish, furiously reduce the *court-bouillon* and turn it into a sauce, thickening with cream. This sauce will be even better if, instead of water, you've used fish stock *(fumet)* made by boiling up fish-bones and fish-heads. You could add some cooked shelled shrimps, and/or some cooked shelled mussels (just opened as for *moules marinières*, page 115); on no account, in Britain, use bottled ones in harsh vinegar. Or, if you are in a *gîte*, put your *court-bouillon* (by now, even more valuable because of the fish you've cooked in it) away in the fridge and have more poached fish the next day, reducing the liquid for sauce on that occasion.

Saucisse à la Sophie

French cooking sausage *(saucisse de Toulouse)* is fine, coiled up and grilled in a folding wire grill on embers or charcoal; and can equally well be shallow-fried in a neat coil. However, some Britons — especially children — accustomed to the bland homogeneous British sausage, do not take kindly at first to the meaty standard French version, composed as it is of coarsely chopped meat and fat. It can be de-fatted and improved as follows:

Equipment: frying-pan and cover (aluminium foil will do); one gas-ring.

Ingredients: *saucisse fraîche*, the quantity you would buy in Britain, but in one length; any wine — red, white, or rosé.

Heat frying-pan with a smear of oil, and rapidly brown your (pricked) sausage on both sides. Then turn down the heat and add wine to come about half-way up the sausage. Cover, and poach gently for twenty minutes or even longer. Serve, throwing away the cooking liquid, which will be very fatty. If there is any sausage over, it will be nice cold.

Rice on the camp-site

Vehement disputes can arise about how to cook rice. But when camping, the "absorption" method is a clear winner, allowing the rice to be prepared with the minimum of gas, and liberating the cooker for other purposes half an hour or more before serving time. Put washed rice in the saucepan, add enough slightly salted water to cover by about a quarter of an inch or a little more (this really depends on the type of rice, and in France you will probably be using unfamiliar French rice from the Camargue). Bring to the boil, and boil furiously for a minute or two, stirring. Cover, and turn the gas to very low. Carry on cooking for five or ten minutes, then take the covered saucepan off the heat and wrap it in a blanket or a sleeping bag or something. You can now leave it for anything from a quarter of an hour to an hour before opening up, fluffing it with a fork and serving. This is much more practical as "padding" on a camp-site than boiled potatoes, with their heavy demands on boiling water.

We like rice as a very plain background to well-flavoured food. But a more luxurious version can be made by first sweating some chopped onion in a little oil or butter, and then putting the uncooked rice in the same saucepan, adding perhaps stock instead of water, and proceeding as above.

Couscous

Equipment: 1 gas-ring (or equivalent); 2 saucepans (one of which can be a pressure-cooker).

Ingredients: a packet of *couscous* (at any *épicerie*; Ferrero is a well-known brand, which can even be got in Britain at about twice the price); stuff for a stew: lots of vegetables, e.g. tomatoes, fresh or canned; little turnips *(navets)*, courgettes, sweet peppers *(poivrons)*, celery; chick peas *(pois chiches)*, dried or canned "au naturel", i.e. in water; onions; carrots, meat of some kind; *harissa* in tube (very cheap).

Couscous is an Arab dish which became popular among French settlers in North Africa *(pieds noirs)*. Essentially, it consists of a farinaceous "padding", couscous itself, which might be considered the North African equivalent of rice; a rather liquid, and certainly unthickened, stew, called *marga*, based traditionally on mutton but for which other meat can be used — or one could even have a vegetarian couscous, and (in *Mediterranean Seafood*) Alan Davidson gives a recipe for a fish couscous from Tunis (the stew, though it should be well-flavoured because of its major ingredients, is not highly seasoned); and a fiery sauce, *harissa*, served in a small bowl, from which one takes teaspoonfuls to mix into one's *marga* until one has achieved the desired degree of hotness. It is served in many French restaurants, typically on Thursday (you will see the notice *"couscous le jeudi"*), usually as a meal in itself, though hors d'oeuvres before and fruit or ice-cream after is pleasant. Not at all *haute cuisine*, but filling family food, and often more successful with families than a curry, as everyone can adjust for himself the violence or mildness of the seasoning.

First make your *marga*. Water perhaps with a stock cube is the medium, not wine. Put in your ingredients in an order based on how long they will take to cook. Chickpeas really are traditional, and we wouldn't want a couscous without them; they will have to be soaked all night, and then they will go in first, and will need a total of a couple of hours. We recommend the holidaymaker to cut corners and use a can of ready-cooked ones, which only need draining and heating — but as they are indestructible they can go in the *marga* at any time. Your meat will then take longest. If you go to the butcher and ask for *de la viande pour un couscous* he will probably suggest breast of mutton, which will need an hour or more. A boiling fowl *(une poularde)* or half would do instead; or some roasting chicken *(poulet,* m.) will give a less well-defined flavour but cook more quickly. Really, any meat will do, but cook it long enough for it to impart a good flavour to the liquid. Add your vegetables in the right order. And carry on simmering without worrying overmuch. When the *marga* is cooked, take it off the gas and keep it warm (if camping, wrap a sleeping bag or a towel round the saucepan or pressure-cooker) and make the couscous, following the directions on the packet or as follows:

Measure out equal volumes of water and couscous — say two cupfuls of each, for four people. Bring the water to the boil in a saucepan, and pour in the couscous, stirring. Continue heating very gently for a minute or two, stirring with a fork and trying to eliminate lumps. Add (optionally) a little butter or oil, and serve.

If you have only one saucepan, which will be in use for the *marga*, you can try putting the couscous in a bowl and pouring the water gradually on to it, stirring; then leave it to swell for a minute or two before having a final attempt at breaking up lumps. With these two quick methods there will inevitably be a lump or two, but they will be quite comestible.

The classical way would have been to steam your couscous above your *marga*. Special double saucepans *(couscoussières)* are sold for this; connoisseurs claim to detect the aromas of the *marga* in the couscous done this way. The "instant" way does perfectly well.

You are now ready to serve. If you have a large serving-dish, pile up a mound of couscous in the centre, and distribute solid items from the *marga* over it. Squirt a teaspoonful or two of *harissa* into a small bowl or saucer, and add some liquid from the *marga* to thin it down. Everybody now helps himself, adding liquid from the *marga* saucepan to sloppify the mess as desired, and cautious amounts of the *harissa* mixture. Spoons will be needed.

A couscous de luxe could include a freshly-grilled skewer of cubes of any kind of meat *(une brochette)* per person; or one or two of those fiery little sausages, *merguez*, grilled — they always give us indigestion, but you may be luckier.

Couscous, as you can see, is not elegant eating. But is can be warmly recommended as a hearty, nourishing and cheap meal, especially for hungry campers.

As with curries and *rijsttafel*, beer is a more suitable drink than wine, because of the seasoning.

You may be tempted by packs of *couscous complet* in the supermarket. These simply consist of a small packet of couscous; a can of stew; and a sachet of *harissa*. They hardly seem worth the price, except perhaps to try the ritual out on the family; you can make a much better *marga* yourself. Remember, when doing the marketing, that it is quite all right, in France, to buy one small turnip, three carrots, etc.

Rabbit fricassée

Equipment: 1 heavy casserole (or biggish saucepan — use an asbestos mat if lightweight; or even a deep frying-pan); 1 gas-ring (or equivalent).

Ingredients:

- 1 rabbit (for 3-6 people, depending on rabbit and people); or half a rabbit for 2-3 people. The butcher will usually be happy to split the rabbit in half lengthways. This is the *lapin d'élevage*, or tame rabbit, usually sold skinned and gutted. Wild rabbits are usually sold in fur and with guts, though they can usually be prepared while you wait and chat;
- 1 onion;
- some cooking oil (ground-nut — *huile d'arachide* — or not too fruity olive oil); a little butter;
- some mushrooms, fresh or canned;
- 10 cl cream (see page 79);
- spoonful flour;
- white wine.

Slice the onion and cut the rabbit into serving pieces. Brown onion and rabbit in oil and butter. When they have coloured, add a spoonful of flour, with salt and pepper, and mix. Add a glass of white wine and simmer gently. How long depends on the age of the rabbit (between $\frac{1}{4}$ of an hour and $2\frac{1}{2}$ hours). Add more wine when necessary to prevent drying up. Test for tenderness occasionally. When almost cooked add mushrooms. If the rabbit is cooked much sooner than you expected, operations can be suspended at this point, and the *fricassée* warmed up again later. Before serving, take out meat and mushrooms, and add the cream to the liquid. Heat gently. Replace meat and mushrooms, and serve. A suitable accompaniment would be something plain — simple boiled potatoes or rice. But if you have only one gas-ring, freshly-made crisp French bread is no hardship — you will need some anyway to mop up the last drop of the delicious sauce, and leave a nicely polished clean plate.

Chicken fricassée

Use the Rabbit Fricassée recipe above. The cooking time will be shorter. The recipe will be better with rabbit; but there is no doubt that the better the chicken (see p. 68) the better the outcome. At the last moment the addition of the juice of half a lemon is recommended.

Chicken à l'armagnac

As above, but: no onion, no flour. Having coloured the chicken pieces add (perhaps) a little paprika, and (certainly) four big spoonfuls of armagnac (or any brandy). Boil vigorously for two minutes. Add a little water to prevent drying out, and simmer until done. After cooking finish with cream, as before.

Oysters

Oysters come in two main kinds: flattish round ones (*huîtres plates*, of which the Belon — and the British Whitstable — are well-known) and the long sort, *Portugaises*. The former cost two or three times as much as the latter. One could buy good *Portugaises*, near the source of production, for about 7 francs a kilo in 1981; there are 12 to 18 in a kilo.

Alan Davidson says: "Lavish your money on these delectable creatures, open them, cool them on a bed of ice and, having sprinkled lemon juice, go to it. It is possible to do other things, such as frying or even grilling them, not to mention including them in steak and kidney pies, but in my belief they are best eaten as they are, and to do otherwise is mistaken and even blameworthy." Amen.

You can however do without the bed of ice (better oysters with no ice than no oysters at all) and even without the squeeze of lemon, though it is a pity not to see them faintly writhing with voluptuous joy as the drops of lemon juice fall... Bread is what we chiefly need — brown for preference (rye, *pain de seigle*, or wholemeal, *pain complet*) but any bread will do; and a bottle of cool light white wine.

"Open them", says Mr. Davidson, just like that. Our first dozen *Portugaises*, opened by the light of nature and with the wrong knife, took us over half an hour and cost blood, sweat and tears. (It was worth it.) The best advice we can give is: ask the oyster merchant to show you. It's quite easy, and he will be happy to oblige. We like to wear a gardening glove on the left hand, or wrap a cloth round it. With the *Portugaise* it is often hard for the amateur to see where the two shells join; so crumble a little shell away at the round end, with kitchen scissors or a stout knife, until a gap is revealed. Then the knife goes in easily.

Forget all about R's in the month. Oysters are good all the year round. Of course they go off quicker in hot weather, but as the oyster should be alive when you eat it, there is no problem — if it lets you open it unresistingly, throw it away without bothering to sniff it.

Just occasionally we do an heretical thing: we make

Grand Central Station oyster soup

Equipment: 1 gas-ring; 1 saucepan.

Ingredients: oysters (the more the better — say up to 6 per person); milk and cream — enough to make up a small soup-bowl per person; seasonings: a few celery leaves *(céleri à couper)*, some mace *(macis)* or nutmeg *(muscade)*, peppercorns *(poivre en grains)*.

Open the oysters, saving the liquid. Bring the liquid to boiling point, with water if there isn't enough liquid for poaching the oysters, add the oysters and poach for a very short time, until, as Mrs. Beeton puts it, the oysters "plump up" a bit — about a quarter of a minute. Put the oysters and the liquid in a bowl and set aside.

Put the seasonings in the milk (we prefer whole mace or biggish lumps of nutmeg — they strain out easily) and put it on the gas to "draw" for about twenty minutes. Then remove the seasonings, add the oysters and some or all of their liquid (taste — after a dry summer in the Étang de Thau the liquid may be very salty); warm up; add the cream; serve (preferably with very plain crisp biscuits, like Carr's Water Biscuits — you can buy big ones, called *pains azymes*, in packets).

Scallop soup

is nice too. Substitute one or two scallops *(coquilles Saint-Jacques)* per person, for the oysters; slice them in two; poach a few minutes in the milk after removal of the seasonings. Finish as above. A little salt will be needed.

Mussels

Excellent mussels grow around the coasts of Britain, but the British are shy of them. Continentals (especially Belgians, with whom *moules et frites* are as popular as they were with Queneau's Zazie) appreciate this delicious cheap food. We first tried *moules marinières* (or *moules à la marinière*) long ago in Le Havre, in a restaurant where we saw great platefuls being devoured by the locals, while we waited for the Southampton boat. We spent our remaining francs on a portion each, and then on another portion each, with bottles of cold white wine, and slept very happily on board with no ill effects. You can rely on the cultivated French mussel, but if you become an addict do not pick your own round the British coasts except in the far wilds — a mussel will filter out a lot of dilute sewage given the chance.

Moules marinières

Equipment: a big saucepan; one gas-ring.

Ingredients: mussels (a kilo for two is by no means too much); shallots or onion (*échalotes, oignon*); parsley (*persil*); white wine.

Elizabeth David warns one against using mussels that float, and one certainly wouldn't use ones that are open and dead.

Scrub the mussels well, and scrape off the "beard" with a knife. For a kilo of mussels, produce a tablespoonful or so of chopped shallot or onion, and put it with some parsley and a glass-full of white wine in the saucepan. Bring to the boil, put in the mussels and put on the lid. Shake the pan from time to time. In a few minutes, when all the mussels have opened, they are ready. Eat, using a mussel-shell as tongs. Slurp up the liquid. Drink cold white wine.

A refinement is slightly to thicken the liquid with a little *beurre manié* (softened butter mashed up with flour) or cream.

Some Mediterranean mussels, after a long dry summer, can be too salty, because of the evaporation from the *parcs* where they are cultivated. So you may have to cheat. Cook as before, but without the wine etc. When they are open, taste the juice. According to its saltiness, throw all or some away. Then add the wine etc. and boil up quickly. But don't overcook mussels or they become tough.

Plump mussels can be good, eaten raw like oysters. Ask the merchant which sort he recommends for this. They are not hard to open with a small vegetable knife — the difficulty is to avoid slicing the body of the mussel in two.

An exotic dish is *Moules à la Sétoise* (from Sète). Buy very big mussels (ask for *moules à farcir*), open them with a knife, stuff with sausage meat, re-close mussels tying each with a piece of string, and braise in a tomato-oil-onion-garlic mixture. Remove string befor serving. Three or four per person is enough. Not a very light dish.

They can be extracted, raw, from their shells, egg-and-breadcrumbed and deep-fried.

Cooked mussels, left over from *moules marinières* (no that this ever happens with us) can be incorporated ir potato salads and other mixed salad dishes.

Grilled fresh sardines

Equipment: a hinged grill; an open-air fire.
Ingredients: really fresh sardines — say 200 gramme per person.
Grilled fresh sardines are a delight. Alan Davidsor

(Mediterranean Seafood) gives some good recipes for fresh sardines, but we think that doing anything other than just grilling them is a pity, unless one is in a set-up where fresh sardines must be eaten seven days a week. (They are very cheap.) The fresh sardine travels badly; if the ones in the market look the worse for wear, don't buy them. If they are in good shape, bright-eyed and smelling nice, give yourself a treat.

Even if you are going to eat them indoors, grill them outside. Oil and juices drip from the sardine as it grills, causing spurts of flame and smoke. You don't want the kitchen (and house) perfumed for the next 24 hours. At a camp-site, there may be a place for barbecues; if not, make sure that it is all right for you to build a fire. Thousands of acres of forest are burned each year by careless people, and the French are justifiably annoyed if ignorant people from wetter climes put their heritage at risk. On the other hand, the French are fond of open-air grilling, so most holiday villas etc. will have a barbecue or at least a place where the right sort of fire can be safely made, and the question *Où est-ce qu'on peut faire des grillades?* (Where can I grill?) will be treated seriously and sympathetically.

Vine-prunings *(sarments de vigne)* are traditional for quick grilling in the Midi, and you might be given some; or you can of course buy charcoal *(charbon de bois,* at the *droguerie)* or find twigs. Wait till the fire has burned down to a steady glow of red embers before you start to cook.

If you are fussy, gut your sardines — easy, since the sardine is so delicate. Just slit the belly with a thumbnail.

Put them in your folding grill, grill them on both sides, and *voilà*. Ideally they should be eaten out of doors and in the fingers — no problem: the scorched skin lifts off and the flesh is sucked from the backbone. A refinement is to gather some herbs from the wilds (thyme, fennel...) and put sprigs in the grill with the sardines. The hinged grill is really essential. It lets you turn the fish without losing them in the fire, and costs very little.

This sort of barbaric eating is fine for summer days in

the south. It is less attractive back home, but worth trying (sprats? fresh pilchards?); your hinged grill will come in handy whenever there is a risk of items falling into the fire. There is a lot to be said for using it by a Highland stream, with trout one has just caught — on a *hot* day.

A note on frying

For camping, deep frying is out: a big saucepan holding a lot of cooking oil is not the sort of thing to have hanging around in a tent, and raising a large volume of oil to cooking temperature takes too much out of a little Camping-Gaz burner. And for short periods in a *gîte*, even if one has been supplied with a deep-fryer and wire basket, an investment in two or three litres of cooking oil may not seem worth while. Here, we would recommend taking your WOK, if you have been switched on to this trendy-in-the-West but traditional Chinese technique. (The French do not of course use the wok, though we have seen some sitting hopefully in the Habitat shop in Montpellier.) With a wok, and a high flame, you need a minimum of cooking oil, even for such bulky things as chips *(frites,* f. — *les chips,* m., are potato crisps, in bags) if you do them in batches; and when you've finished you pour the surplus oil into a jar and save it for next time. We bought, in Catalonia, just across the border, two practical strainer-lidded jars for this purpose, one labelled CARN (meat) and the other PEIX (fish), for keeping the two "second-hand" oils separate — not that Catalans use woks, but they have a similar small-quantity deep-frying system. Two empty cans serve just as well.

Watch out when you buy your oil. Olive oil is dear, and there are all sorts of other oils in the shops, of which perhaps ground-nut oil *(huile d'arachide)* is best for frying. Some oils will not take the heat required for frying; look at the small print on the bottle: *huile pour assaisonnement* is for use cold, on salads etc.; *huile pour friture* is for frying.

If equipped for deep or medium deep frying, buy in the market *petite friture*: tiny fish no bigger than your little finger, like whitebait (sometimes called *joël* or *jol* in the South). Wash, *dry*, flour very lightly, and fry to the desired degree of crispness. Eat whole, with a squeeze of lemon; don't let them get luke-warm, never try to keep them warm — they should sizzle on the plate, straight from the pan. Do the same with thumb-sized baby octopuses *(seppions, suppions, sépioles*, and other similar names) — bought cleaned *(nettoyés)* if possible, otherwise you will need to remove eyes, ink-sac, hidden beak, guts and tiny "bone". This is no trouble with their larger relations, but it takes ages with a pound of babies. Watch out — they splutter.

Steak

If you have always grilled your steak, and you are now camping in a *gîte* with no proper grill, you can of course grill it over a charcoal or wood-ember fire (if there is a place for one). We are fond of this barbaric method of outdoor cooking and eating, but feel that steak represents too considerable an investment to be risked in this way (no one minds if just one or two sardines catch alight, or if a bit of sausage falls into the sand). Do not be disdainful of fried steak; we think it better than grilled, if done this way:

Make a good heavy frying-pan very hot, with just a smear of oil in it (*not* butter — it will turn black and be nasty). Put in your steak. After a minute, turn it (with steak-tongs if you have them — don't puncture it). The side you have turned up should be an appetising brown. Reduce the heat somewhat, and watch. When tiny beads of juice begin to exude, your steak is *à point*: pink, not red, in the centre; you have cooked it too long for it to be *saignant* (bleeding, or very rare); for *bien cuit*, or brown in the middle, carry on a minute or so longer. (Exact times

cannot be given — the time varies according to the square
of the thickness). Transfer steak to plate, which if possible
you will have warmed. Now pour into the pan a small
glass-full of the red wine you are going to drink (and
should have already opened to let it "breathe"). Turn the
heat right up, and stir around, scraping up any coagulated
meat-juices. When there is no more than a spoonful of
liquid left — the rest having boiled away — take the pan off
the heat, swirl in a little softened butter, pour this delicious *jus* over the steak, and there you are. The butter can
be omitted.

Of course in a good *gîte* you can make *sauce béarnaise* —
the best of all sauces with steak, and many other things
(see any good cookery book). But when camping, the
tubes of alleged "sauce béarnaise" made by Benedicta are
quite good, though of course not the genuine article.
The same firm makes a good bottled (and tubed)
"mayonnaise" — only a substitute for the fresh thing, but
quite different from the British bottled variety. However,
real mayonnaise can perfectly well be made when
camping: just speak firmly to the cook.

A modest banquet

Some people have the idea that France is terribly expensive. The dinner below can cost less than £6 for four
people (wine included) at 1981 prices. It can be served
half-an-hour after coming home to the tent (or to the *gîte*
— but we have deliberately thought in terms of camping,
simple work and one-burner cookery).

> Oysters or hors d'oeuvre.
>> Chilled white wine.
> Simple beef (see page 105).
>> Red wine.
> *Salade verte* (i.e. a lettuce).
> Cheese.

Bananes flambées.
   "Champagne" (i.e. cheap sparkling wine).

The "simple beef" should have been prepared earlier,
and left in the tent in a pressure cooker with the lid
securely fixed (in case of wandering dogs etc.).

The white wine and the fizzy wine should be in the
cold-box, with a freshly-refrozen "thermal pack", or some
ice from the camp shop; or attached to a piece of string
and immersed in a cool river.

Put the stew on to re-heat, on a gentle flame with an
asbestos mat.

If there are people who declared, at marketing-time,
that they would prefer hors d'oeuvres to oysters, prepare
what has taken their fancy in the way of *crudités* (raw
vegetables) — perhaps grated carrot, sliced fennel bulb,
tomatoes, radishes, a variety of olives, green and black
(the olive-merchant will cheerfully put you up 100 or 200
grammes of mixed varieties), with a slice or two of *saucisson sec*; or what has tempted them in the way of ready-
prepared hors d'oeuvres at the *charcuterie* — this may
however make you exceed the budget suggested.

Wash lettuce and shake dry.

Open the oysters, produce a lemon, open the white
wine, and cut the bread. Eat. Drink.

Clean plates with paper napkins. Serve stew, with bread
and red wine.

Polish plates with bread. Serve lettuce, with olive oil
and wine vinegar.

Polish plates with bread. See what there is in the way of
cheese. More red wine.

Polish plates with bread. Melt a little butter in frying-
pan, cook bananas (sliced lengthways in half) gently until
softish, sprinkle with sugar, pour on two or three table-
spoons of cheap brandy or rum, set alight in the pan;
serve, while someone else has opened the fizzy wine.

Optional extra: relax with coffee, a cigar and some
more brandy while someone else does the washing-up.

Our costing is based on: a litre of ordinary white wine,

at 4 francs or less the litre (exclusive of bottle, on which
there is a deposit); a litre or more of red wine, bought *en
vrac* (see page 97) at about 3 francs the litre; a bottle of
mousseux at 7,50 F. Brandy or rum from stock.

2 kilos of oysters *(Portugaises)*, 14 francs. Beef
20 francs. Lettuce 1 franc. Bananas 4 francs or less. Oil,
vinegar, sugar from stock. Cheese perhaps from stock;
but let us say a total of 10 francs for cheese and all the
bread. This comes to about 65 francs.

It would be interesting to work out the cost of the same
menu in Britain... This brings us to Harris's Law of Com-
parative Shopping Costs, which states that Mrs. A's shopping list, established for country A on the basis of what
represents good value there, costs a lot more in country
B; while, conversely, Mrs. B's shopping list, established
for country B on the basis of what represents good value
there, costs a lot more in country A.

Your French neighbours, by the way, would not
consider the above to be a banquet, modest or otherwise,
but an ordinary reasonable healthy meal. We, on the other
hand, would be moderately happy to do without either
the oysters or the beef, to substitute fresh peaches for
flaming bananas, and to have a glass of dessert wine with
them instead of the *mousseux*.

Coping with the British child

This is not a chapter on child-management. All we aim to
do is give advice on feeding your little ones, and on
getting rid of them.

We sometimes give talks to French schoolchildren who
are going to visit Britain. We say: rejoice! No long boring
meals during which you have to shut up and listen to
tedious grown-up conversation — just small plainish
affairs which you can gobble up in twenty minutes flat, or
even less. But won't we get hungry? they ask. No! You
will have had an egg and lovely cornflakes for breakfast!

soon after, there will be elevenses; half-way through the afternoon it's tea-time; and every true British child expects at least two ounces of confectionery per day, and regular ice-creams; and when you are hungry, factory-made cakes and biscuits, if not as nice as the ones from the *pâtisserie*, are cheap, cheap, cheap... They usually come back full of enthusiasm for the much-maligned British cuisine; they just love baked beans on toast.

The boot is on the other foot, for the British child in France. You can of course supply it with daily hand-made chocolates, and marzipan sweets made from real almonds and real egg-yolks, but it will cost a fortune. French children get these things only on Sundays, if then. If you are lucky, your child may show an enlightened interest in *moules marinières* and *tripes à la mode de Caen*, and willingly sit like a normal well-disciplined French child through the lunch and dinner ritual at the restaurant — and may even discover his own specialities (one of us became a francophile at the age of four because of *vol-au-vent*; with the other, at five, it was chocolate *soufflé*); but the average small Briton is better off under a self-catering regime (and see SNACKS on page 42 and CAFÉS on page 45). After all, if baked beans are what it likes, a couple of dozen cans in the boot of the car will keep it happy, and save you money for serious grown-up luxuries. Make your own *sauce béarnaise*, but do not blush at producing a bottle of tomato sauce. The French equivalent of canned baked beans is canned *cassoulet*: much dearer, and not so blandly acceptable to the childish palate. Canned rice pudding can be got at about the same price as at home, but cornflakes cost something shocking. A stock of non-melting cheap confectionery will come in handy. We are not suggesting that *you* should eat this sort of stuff — but if your offspring will eat Instant Mash, and are going to be difficult about *les gloires de la cuisine française*, why not pander to them *and* economise?

If you are in France during term-time, French schools will accept your children, free! (if there is room).

Obviously this is not worth trying if you will be there for only a short period; but we have known it to be very successful from all points of view (even the child's) with people staying put for a couple of months. The younger the child, the better — there are perhaps too many complications with curriculum (and self-consciousness) at the secondary stage. We know one couple, on a term's "sabbatical" leave, who sent their *six* children, aged from five to eleven, to a village school — the percentage of Scots children in the school went well into double figures. The nursery department at that school was not successful with another academic lady's three-year-old, but it was very happy all day long at the nursery school in the nearest town, two miles away. Our own one-teacher village school normally numbers about eight on the roll; to which for one term were added two large eleven-and twelve-year-old Norwegian girls, daughters of an architect friend of ours who spent a winter in the Midi, working with his hands as an alternative to a nervous breakdown — the girls knew no French at first, but loved it: the work was easy (the French children being small) and they soon acquired an impressive fluency, with of course a beautiful *accent du Midi*.

The French school year is the shortest in Europe, but the school day is the longest.

Doctors and insurance

les médecins (m., whether male or female) *et l'assurance* (f.)

Doctors are much the same on both sides of the Channel. French ones have more experience of liver complaints, British ones of duodenal ulcers, because of differences in the way of life, but otherwise ailments and their treatment are not dissimilar.

There are two points worth making, however.

First, there are more doctors in France. The profession is better paid than in Britain, and attracts more recruits. In many areas of France the doctors complain that they are too thick on the ground. Thus you are likely to spend less time in the waiting room, and more time in the consulting room. Do not hesitate to ask the doctor to visit you — our own doctor tell us he prefers to do this, as he gets paid more and it makes an agreeable diversion.

Second: your French doctor is much more likely to prescribe a *suppositoire*. This is a "pill" that you stick up your arse. We make this brutally clear, for there are many stories — some alas true — of British tourists who have tried to swallow *suppositoires*, not having fully understood the instructions. A most unwise procedure. In Britain, suppositories are usually only prescribed for affections of the lower end of the alimentary canal. The French, logically enough, consider that as the active ingredient of many remedies is absorbed in the bowel, one should take the shortest route there, leaving the sensitive stomach untroubled; so they prescribe, in suppository form, substances and quantities that it would be better not to take by mouth. We have been quite converted, since long ago, when one of us, afflicted by a crippling headache, and unable to keep down on an empty stomach the British pain-killing pills that we had brought with us, took a French chemist's advice and inserted a quite magical *suppositoire*.

If however you absolutely refuse this method of ingestion, tell the doctor: *"Je ne supporte pas les suppositoires"*, and he will prescribe the next best thing. Attempts may be made to take your temperature by the same orifice; to avoid this, you should have taken your temperature with the British clinical thermometer you have brought with you; you can then tell the doctor how many centigrade degrees of fever you have. As a degree fahrenheit is about half a degree centigrade, just see how many degrees fahrenheit you are above normal, and halve them. For example, a fahrenheit temperature of 100·4° is two degrees fahrenheit "up" from normal, 98·4°; so you will tell the doctor you have *"un degré de fièvre"*. This is much simpler than trying to subtract 32, divide by 9 and multiply by 5. But if you are very ill, you will not be able to resist these attentions. *Ce n'est que le premier pas qui coûte.* It has been suggested by the French that the well-known British squeamishness in these matters is caused by the influence of Protestantism. We have not yet been able to see the connection.

We shall not attempt a medical dictionary. But a little reassurance: if you hear the words *anthrax* (m.) or *angine* (f.) bandied around, they do *not* mean anthrax or angina pectoris (not in ordinary speech, that is). The former is a sort of boil, the latter just a sore throat. While one hopes to avoid these minor ailments, they are more frequent and less alarming than their names suggest to the Briton. (Proper anthrax is *le charbon*, or *anthrax malin*, and luckily extremely rare; angina is *angine de poitrine*, the word *angine* by itself being the sore throat.)

It is wise to be covered by medical and accident insurance. If you have taken out a "holiday" policy with a British company, you will ask the doctor for a receipt (standard charge for a consultation in 1981: 60 francs) and get one from the chemist too. A hospital may want to see your insurance policy when you are admitted, to verify that they will get their fees.

The snag with the usual holiday insurance policy is that there is an upper limit to the sum assured, and that very often "pre-existing ailments and defects" are not covered. This makes it well worth while going to the trouble of getting a Form E 111 from the Department of Health and Social Security. Armed with this, you are in the same position as a French person under his system of National Insurance. The sky is the limit for expense, and there are no problems about pre-existing ailments. This is one of the advantages of being in the Common Market.

The French "National Health" system is different from the British. Oh dear yes... When you see the doctor, he will (if you ask) give you a form, the *feuille de maladie*. The D.H.S.S. leaflet SA 36/1979 "Medical Treatment for Visitors to other E.E.C. Countries", tells you to go to the *caisse primaire* first, to get a *feuille de maladie* and a list of doctors. No need. All ordinary doctors (but not highly fashionable and expensive ones) will give you a *feuille de maladie*.

You will pay him there and then the full price for the consultation or visit. If he gives a prescription, you will take this, with the *feuille de maladie*, to the chemist. The chemist will charge you the full price for the items prescribed, and will enter them on the *feuille*. He or you will detach from each package or bottle a sticky label, called the *vignette* (it gives the name and price of the item) and stick it on the *feuille* in the space provided. If that is the lot — that is, if you are now cured — all you now have to do is to get yourself reimbursed for these expenses (or rather, for part of them). But if you need another consultation, and perhaps more items from the chemist, the further expense can go on the same *feuille de maladie*.

The next step is to apply to the local *caisse d'assurance primaire*. This office will be in the nearest large town; the doctor or chemist will tell you where. They will want the *feuille de maladie* (with the *vignettes* affixed) and the relevant prescription. They will also want to see your

Form E 111, but do not give it up — unless you are absolutely sure you will not need any more medical attention before you touch British shores. With luck, you could be in and out in half an hour. And in the fullness of time — say a couple of months — you will receive, back home, a money order. For an ordinary minor affair, dealt with by doctor and prescription, you will recover about three-quarters of the cost. Similarly for dental emergencies (for *doctor*, above, read *dentist*). For something major and expensive you will get back more, or even all. If you are wheeled into hospital just wave your Form E 111 at them, or get someone else to, and relax.

The Department of Health and Social Security will give you a Form E 111 (after you have filled up their Form CM 1 — that's life) if you are *employed*. Your Form E 111 covers yourself and your dependents. But if you are self employed or non-employed, your entitlement to a Form E 111 may depend on whether you have previously paid contributions as an employed person (or, if you are a widow, and receiving widow's benefit, whether your late husband had paid such contributions). The D.H.S.S. leaflet SA 30, of January 1981, tries to clarify the position of people who are not employed, and nearly succeeds; but a visit to the local D.H.S.S. office is clearly indicated.

Being *un*employed is not the same as being *non*-employed. The non-employed are persons of leisure, and the retired. If you have got the "old age" pension you are all right, but if you have retired before getting it, that is before 65 if you are a man, or 60 if you are a woman, you can get a Form E 111 only if you have paid enough contributions to entitle you to a full-rate "state" pension when you do reach that age. But the unemployed count as employed... We know an ex-headmaster, in receipt of a teacher's pension — which is not a "state" pension within the meaning of the act — who for some reason had not paid enough contributions for a full-rate "old age" pension, and who is under 65. He went in at one door, registered as unemployed (without claiming benefit, and

without having another headmastership pressed upon
him); then, having attained that respectable status, went
in at the other door, got his Form E 111 and departed for
six months in France with all his pre-existing ailments
and defects.

Of course all this fuss and bother with the *caisse
primaire* and the vignettes and what-not is a confounded
nuisance, especially as you don't get all your money back.
We strongly advise those coming for a short stay to adopt
the belt-and-braces tactic : take out a modest holiday
insurance policy with a British company, and use that for
all it covers. (Don't forget the doctor's and chemist's
receipts, and the prescriptions.) But have your E 111 as
well, for what your holiday policy doesn't cover.

If you are settling in France as an employed person, you
will be covered as such. You will have to check on this
beforehand with your employer and the bureaucracy.

If you are settling as a non-employed person, you can
get cover under the French scheme, by making fairly
large voluntary payments (1108 francs per quarter, in
1981 — more, if your income was very high) which cover
yourself *and your dependants*; you should check on this
with the bureaucracy quite early in your stay, as if you
delay too long you may not be entitled to become an
assuré volontaire. If you have no dependants, you might
consider the "subscription" too high for only one person,
especially if you think you will be able to belt back to
Britain when you feel an expensive illness coming on.
This is a matter of temperament.

If you have a British "old age" pension and settle in
France, you should be able to be covered free; but see the
note on page 138 and check early, with the bureaucracies
of both countries. (You are entitled to receive your British
"old age" pension if you settle in France, together with all
later increases — this is not the case if you settle in some
other countries.)

If you suffer a serious accident or suddenly become gravely ill, without having adequate insurance cover, you are in an awkward situation. However, failure to assist a person in danger is a criminal offence in France, and this applies to doctors as well as everybody else. No hospital or doctor will let you bleed to death. But you had better contact the nearest British consulate or vice-consulate (a list is on page 139) as soon as possible. They will do their best to help you to get into touch with someone in Britain who can guarantee that you will pay, or will advise you on other proceedings. When you are on your feet again, if you have not been able to pay the probably huge bills (hospitals can cost £100 a day...) you will have to sign some sort of undertaking to do so later. The consul may advise you that having a nurse sent out from Britain to escort you home for continued treatment is the best solution, and his staff may be able to help in arranging this. The consulate does *not* have funds at its disposal to pay your bills.

To repeat: it is folly not to be insured. The fact that in Britain everyone is insured for all medical risks, automatically, without having to do anything about it, tends to make some people forget that this only applies on British soil. In France everybody is insured in one way or another, but less automatically — they have to do something about it. So should people who visit France or settle there.

Buying a house

Time was when property in rural France could be picked up for a song. A friend of ours bought a nice twenty-rooms-plus-dungeons château, with southern aspect and view for miles, for about £2,500 in 1960; and in those days £100 could buy a big dilapidated hovel, which £500 or so could turn into an acceptable country house with all mod. cons. No longer. The Dordogne has been colonised by readers of Freda White; in the season the *épiceries* of the Lot resound with the accents of Sloane Square; the Dutch have taken over the Ardèche, the Germans are in the Camargue, Laurence Durrell has the Gard; and every successful Frenchman wants a *résidence secondaire* in the country.

However, except for brand-new houses, you can find reasonable bargains: that is, if you choose an area that has not yet gone up in the world (detected by the absence of Parisian or Belgian pseudo-rustic "good taste" on cottage exteriors). In this case, you may possibly make an excellent investment. There is still a movement from the country to the town; farmers' children now go to university and then work in the big city; and other farmers do well for themselves and build new villas on the outskirts of their villages. They may need to sell their old houses to finance the new ones, though wealthier city dwellers who inherit country property may well keep it on for a holiday house or simply as a hedge against inflation.

Word-of-mouth and the grape-vine *(le téléphone arabe)* remain the best means of pursuing a house-hunt, for there are many properties which the owner has not decided to put into the hands of an agent, but might seriously consider selling if an offer were made to him. But of course there are agents *(agents immobiliers)* who will gladly show you what they've got on their books. They do not put up big "For Sale" boards as in Britain. When you visit a village there is usually no visible evidence of what is, or might perhaps be, for sale. There are advertisements in the local papers. And British agents who specialise in this sort of thing. But generally speaking, if what you want is a near-ruin in Paradise for £5,000, you had better ask around. The *mairie* in a small village will be an excellent place to start your investigations; and the *patron* of the café might know someone who might be persuaded to cash in on a cottage that has been empty for years.

Some Britons are naïve about the weather. The words "the South of France" have a magical ring: lotus-eating in the Garden of Eden... The over-populated coastal strip known as the Côte d'Azur is one thing, but a picturesque spot in the Massif Central may have colder winters than anywhere in England, even though it's three-quarters of the way down the map of France. Beware also of statistics about the weather. The Languedoc, for example, is a beautiful region, houses for holidays and retirement can still be found at a moderate price, and we love it. The statistics show that Montpellier has more hours of sunshine per year and fewer rainy days than Nice; it enjoys the typical Mediterranean climate: mild winters, dry summers, rain mainly in big buckets on a few spring and autumn days (the total rainfall being about the same as London's). But averages are made by adding things up and dividing the result, and tell one nothing about whether all the things are about the same size or whether they differ wildly. In the Languedoc, about 300 days in the year stick close to the norm, and a couple of months (on the average!) are marked by wildly differing catastrophes: disastrous droughts; spectacular floods; frosts in May; and winds uprooting trees... The prevailing winds are northerly *(le mistral, le terral, la tramontane)*. In winter and spring it blows into our back garden about one day in eight (on the average...) and it feels like the North Pole — but just outside our front door there's about two square yards where on the same day we can sit and sun-bathe, until half past one, when the sun disappears round the corner. The orientation of one's house is a major factor and deserves full investigation from the potential house-buyer.

When you and the owner have agreed on a price, you will not be "gazumped" in the two or three-month interval before the house is legally yours. Both of you will immediately, at the *notaire*'s or the agent's, sign a private contract, called a *sous-seing privé* (i.e. "under private seal") in which you bind yourself — and your heirs and successors, in case you suddenly drop dead — to buy the house for the price stated, and he binds himself likewise. Then the *notaire* will get on with the job, and some weeks or months later you (or a proxy whom you will appoint) will hand over the cash, and all is over (bar the plumbing).

To the price you agree to pay to the seller of the house you will have to add 10 % (or less, depending on the value of the house) as fees and expenses. (In some *départements* the agent's fee is payable by the seller, in some by the buyer, and in others it is divided between the two.)

You may be asked to take part in some funny business about the *prix réel* and the *prix déclaré*. Quite often buyer and seller agree on the price of the house, and this figure, the "real" price, goes down on the *sous-seing privé*, which is a private contract. Then they agree on what they will state as the "declared", or official, price, which goes down on the official documents legalising the transfer. The difference between the two is then a matter of a cash transaction, made at the moment of payment of the official price. This fiddle saves the buyer a little money, because some fees are based on the declared price. It may save the seller more money, since capital gains tax is payable on profits made on the sale of a *résidence secondaire* (but not on the sale on one's main, or only, house). Inflation and improvements are taken into consideration, so there may not be much in this, unless when the seller originally bought the house the declared price was very low.

Until recently one then had a wearisome process to undergo with the Bank of England, in order to get permission to exchange one's sterling via the "dollar pool", paying a premium to do so. This is no longer the case. Your British bank will advise you of the formalities, and deal with most of them. It is convenient to have opened an "external" bank account at a French bank near the house you are buying. The British bank will then transfer the funds. (With an external account, you can pay in to your credit only foreign — e.g. British — currency, not French francs. But you can of course withdraw from it in francs. France has not yet liberated its exchange control regulations to the extent that Britain has. But if you become a resident in France, rather than an occasional visitor with a holiday house, you can have a normal account.)

The subject of alterations, extensions, plumbing and so forth is beyond the scope of this book. Suffice it to say that we know many "foreigners" who have bought houses in France (mostly in the Midi). We have heard very few complaints about the quality of work done (and much praise, especially when small family firms of builders have been employed); many groans about broken promises, or semi-promises, about *when* the work would be done (especially when the owners were far away, and had no local friends to chivvy the *maçons*); and — so far — no complaints about honesty.

You will of course insure your house, probably with the local branch of a French insurance company. As for the amount to insure it for, things are simpler in France: there is no need to worry each year whether you have insured it for the right amount. In France your house is insured for the cost of rebuilding it. So one starts at a suitable figure (based on the floor area if the house is built of normal materials in a normal manner) and this goes up every year, being multiplied by an officially agreed coefficient based on current building costs. So, of course, does the premium. (If building and other costs ever went down, so would the amount the house was insured for, and the premium; but if that sort of thing happened there would be additional risks from pigs trying out their wings.)

Local taxes *(taxes foncières* and *taxes d'habitation,* i.e. rates) seem on the whole less formidable than in Britain.

The French Consulates in Britain will give you full information about customs formalities when moving goods and furniture to France. No duty will normally have to be paid, but a lot of forms will have to be filled up.

Emigrating

We cannot help you weigh up
of emigrating to France, wheth
Self-catering holidays may have
whether you would be hap
established. Plenty of people
you should be able to meet som
about their experiences. Your b
you with copies of the Bank of I
leaflets from the Inland Reve
Health and Social Security also
You will need all this up-to-d
official British point of view o
Market country. The nearest
helpful in giving you the late

Perhaps however it is worth
about the special, but not unu
of retiring to France on a pen
income. Regulations etc. may
the general attitude and tradi
in the matter of taxation an
stay broadly the same.

From the British point of
you can put the money you
where in the wide world. Fro
if you bring it into France yo
getting it out again. This
what Geneva or Zurich can d
which will have links with S
will advise you.

You will be better off pas
There is a double-taxation a
Britain, so tax deducted
investments will be refun

Inspector of Foreign Dividends (your previous British tax inspector will transfer your case to him). Not only is French income tax lower, but the French encourage the small saver. Thus, assuming that you have brought some capital into France, in 1980 you could get the first 3,000 francs interest p.a. on *obligations* (fixed-interest investments), free of tax; and the first 3,000 francs p.a. of dividends on *actions* (shares); so that was 6,000 francs disregarded for tax purposes. Then there are other *abattements*, or chunks of income to be disregarded for tax purposes — your French bank manager, or a French accountant, or even your local French tax inspector, will advise you. Well, the figures may be different in future years. But to give a rough idea of the income tax liability: on their 1980 income of about £4,000, a retired English couple we know had to pay *no* income tax. Their "rates" came to about £60 on a modest well-equipped house. But they also paid about £400 voluntary social security payments, for health insurance. Later, when the husband is 65 and thus gets his British "old age" pension (or when his wife becomes a widow and gets her British widow's pension), the social security health insurance should be free.

All this is vague and approximate; but it remains true that the French are kind to a modest amount of investment income, have a low income tax and raise their money through V.A.T. Any money you spend on insulating your house, or installing solar heating, can be deducted from your taxable income (in one go, in one year).

The French authorities look benevolently on Britons establishing themselves in France. They can be a little difficult in the case of young hairy types who look as though they might have something to do with international terrorist movements and appear to have no visible means of support. But otherwise, there will be no difficulty about getting a *permis de séjour* (after a reckless expenditure in small passport-size photographs). After about a year's residence they will give you a French driving licence without a test, on the same terms as your existing British one.

One is never cut off from one's British friends and relations if one lives in France, especially in the South. They turn up.

NOTE: It seems that, under present regulations, one is entitled to become a voluntary contributor for French health insurance only if one applies within six months of settling in France; and that if one later reaches 65 and becomes entitled to the British "old age" pension, one would get free French health insurance only if one were already a voluntary contributor. Thus, even if one is sure that one's health is so robust that the French voluntary contributions would come to more than one would ever have to pay to doctors, dentists and hospitals in any one year, it would nevertheless be worth paying them if one is within sight of one's sixties, since a few years' payment would entitle one to free insurance from 65 onwards. But we repeat that Common Market and Anglo-French regulations are complex, and liable to modification. In such an important matter one should get the latest information, both from the (British) Department of Health and Social Security and from the French Consulate (or French Social Security offices if one is already in France).

British consulates

The staff of British consulates and vice-consulates are helpful and efficient at dealing with serious enquiries and emergencies. (They are also adept at fending off professional lame ducks.)

This is the current list of consulates and vice-consulates:

BORDEAUX. — 15 cours de Verdun, tel. 52.28.35.

BOULOGNE-SUR-MER. — c/o British Railways, gare maritime, tel. 30.25.11.

CALAIS. — 9-11 rue Félix-Cadras, tel. 34.45.48.

DUNKERQUE. — 6 place de l'Yser, tel. 66.11.98.

ÉPERNAY. — 37 avenue de Champagne, tel. 51.31.02.

LE HAVRE. — 9 quai George-V, tel. 42.27.47.

LILLE. — 11 square Dutilleul, tel. 52.87.90.

LYON. — 24 rue Childebert, tel. 37.59.67.

MARSEILLE. — 24 avenue du Prado, tel. 53.43.32.

NANTES. — 6 rue Lafayette, tel. 48.57.47.

PARIS. — 109 rue du Faubourg-Saint-Honoré, tel. 266.91.42.

PERPIGNAN. — 10 rue Grande-des-Fabriques, tél. 34.56.99.

The inventory - l'inventaire

Some words—for fixtures etc.—which will not figure on an inventory are included, as they will crop up in dealing with the landlord.

When making enquiries about household articles, *le machin* and *le truc* (see page 24) can be useful.

ALLUME-GAZ *(m.)* gas-lighter.

AMPOULE *(f.)* electric light bulb (- À BAÏONNETTE, with bayonet base; - À VIS, with screw base).

ASSIETTE CREUSE *(f.)* soup plate.

ASSIETTE PLATE *(f.)* dinner plate.

BALAI *(m.)* broom.

BALAI *(m.)* ÉPONGE squeezy mop.

BALANCE *(f.)* household scales.

BASSIN *(m.)* basin.

BASSINE *(f.)* basin.

BATTEUR *(m.)* À ŒUFS egg beater.

BEURRIER *(m.)* butter dish.

BOÎTE *(f.)* À PAIN bread box.

BOL (À DÉJEUNER) *(m.)* bowl (instead of cup) for breakfast coffee.

BOUILLOIRE *(f.)* kettle.

BOUTEILLE *(f.)* (or CYLINDRE, *m.)* DE GAZ cooking gas cylinder.

BROC *(m.)* large jug.

BROCHETTE *(f.)* skewer.

CAFETIÈRE *(f.)* coffee pot.

CARAFE *(f.)* decanter.

CASSEROLE *(f.)* saucepan.

CENDRIER *(m.)* ashtray.

CHAUFFE-EAU *(m.)* water heater, geyser.

CHIFFON *(m.)* duster, rag.

CINTRE *(m.)* coat-hanger.

COCOTTE-MINUTE *(f.)* pressure-cooker.

COIN D'ÉVIER *(m.)* sink tidy.

COQUETIER *(m.)* egg-cup.

CORBEILLE *(f.)* À PAIN bread basket.

COUPERET *(m.)* meat cleaver.

COUTEAU *(m.)* knife; - DE CUISINE, kitchen knife; - À DÉCOU-
   PER, carving knife; - À HUÎTRES, oyster knife.

COUVERCLE *(m.)* lid.

COUVERT *(m.)* set of knife, fork and spoon.

COUVERTURE *(f.)* blanket.

CUILLER, CUILLÈRE *(f.)* spoon.

CUISINIÈRE *(f.)* cooker.

CUVETTE *(f.)* bowl, basin.

DÉBOUCHOIR *(m.)* rubber plunger.

DESCENTE *(f.)* DE LIT bedside mat.

DESSOUS *(m.)* DE BOUTEILLE bottle-mat, coaster; - DE PLAT,
   D'ASSIETTE, table-mat; - DE VERRE, coaster.

DRAP *(m.)* sheet.

EAU *(f.)* DE JAVEL household disinfectant bleach.

ÉCHELLE *(f.)* ladder.

ÉCUMOIRE *(f.)* skimming-ladle.

ÉDREDON *(m.)* eiderdown.

ÉGOUTTOIR *(m.)* drying-up rack; basket of deep frier.

ENTONNOIR *(m.)* funnel.

ÉPLUCHE-LÉGUMES *(m.)* vegetable peeler.

ÉPONGE *(f.)* sponge.

ESSUIE-VAISSELLE *(m.)* drying-up towel.

FAIT-TOUT *(m.)* stew-pan.

FER À REPASSER *(m.)* iron (for laundry).

FOUET *(m.)* À ŒUFS egg whisk.

GRILLE-PAIN *(m.)* toaster.

HACHOIR *(m.)* chopping knife.

HUILIER *(m.)* oil and vinegar cruet.

LAVETTE *(f.)* saucepan brush, washing-up mop.

LIT *(m.)* bed; GRAND -, double bed; - POUR UNE PERSONNE,
   single bed; - PLIANT, folding bed; LITS SUPERPOSABLES,
   bunks (but on trains and boats, bunks are COUCHETTES).

LOUCHE *(f.)* ladle.

LOYER *(m.)* rent (for villa etc.).

MARMITE *(f.)* stew pan.

MATELAS *(m.)* mattress.

MAZOUT *(m.)* fuel oil as used for space heaters with chimneys.

MOULE *(m.)* À GÂTEAUX cake mould.

MOULIN *(m.)* À CAFÉ coffee grinder; - À LÉGUMES, vegetable mill, "mouli".

OREILLER *(m.)* pillow.

OUVRE-BOÎTE *(m.)* tin-opener.

PANIER *(m.)* À BOUTEILLES bottle-carrier; - À SALADE salad shaker.

PAPIER *(m.)* HYGÉNIQUE, - TOILETTE toilet paper.

PASSOIRE *(f.)* strainer, colander.

PELLE *(f.)* shovel, scoop.

PLANCHE *(f.)* À DÉCOUPER carving board.

PLAT *(m.)* dish; - À FOUR, - ALLANT AU FOUR, baking dish.

PLATEAU *(m.)* tray.

POÊLE *(m.)* stove (for space heating; a cooking-stove is UNE CUISINIÈRE).

POÊLE, *f.* frying-pan.

POIVRIER *(m.)* pepper-pot, pepper-mill.

PORTE-BALAI W.-C. *(m.)* lavatory brush holder.

PORTE-SAVON *(m.)* soap dish.

POUBELLE *(f.)* dustbin.

PRESSE-CITRON *(m.)* lemon squeezer.

RAMASSE-COUVERTS *(m.)* cutlery tray.

RAMASSE-MIETTES *(m.)* crumb tray, crumb scoop.

RÂPE-FROMAGE *(m.)* cheese grater.

RÉCHAUD *(m.)* boiling-ring.

ROULEAU *(m.)* À PÂTE, - À PÂTISSERIE rolling-pin.

SALADIER *(m.)* salad bowl.

SALIÈRE *(f.)* salt cellar.

SAUCIÈRE *(f.)* sauce boat.

SAUTEUSE *(f.)* frying-pan.

SEAU *(m.)* bucket.

SÉCHOIR *(m.)* clothes horse.

SERPILLIÈRE *(f.)* floor-cloth.

SERVICE *(m.)* DE TABLE dinner service, dinner set.

SERVIETTE *(f.)* DE TABLE table napkin.

SERVIETTE-ÉPONGE *(f.)* bath towel, Turkish towel.
SOUCOUPE *(f.)* saucer.
SOUPIÈRE *(f.)* soup tureen.
TABLE *(f.)* À REPASSER ironing table.
TAPIS *(m.)* carpet, mat.
TASSE *(f.)* cup.
TIRE-BOUCHON *(m.)* corkscrew.
TORCHON *(m.)* floorcloth, dishcloth, duster.
TRAVERSIN *(m.)* bolster.
VAISSELLE *(f.)* crockery; FAIRE LA -, do the washing-up.
VASE *(m.)* vase; - DE NUIT, chamber pot.
VERRE *(m.)* glass; - GRADUÉ, graduated measure.
VINAIGRIER *(m.)* vinegar cruet.

Index

Where several consecutive pages deal with one subject, the number of the first page only is given.